FRANCES R. HORWICH
(Miss Frances)

THE MAGIC OF BRINGING UP YOUR CHILD

McGraw-Hill Book Company, Inc.

NEW YORK   TORONTO   LONDON

To Harvey

CONTENTS

❋⤙☿⤛❋⤙☿⤛❋⤙☿⤛❋⤙☿⤛❋⤙☿⤛

If I were a child again . . .

Once upon a time, you too were a child.

I can see you laughing at me. "Of course I was a child once!"

Of course—but do you remember how it really was? Think of yourself as the little girl or the little boy you once were.

Bring out those funny snapshots, or the mementos you have kept to help you remember.

A host of people and incidents arise from the mists of memory. . . .

You think of your parents in those early years. Were they understanding? What mistakes that they made are you trying to avoid in bringing up your own child? Don't load on Mother and Dad the blame for every disappointment and painful disillusion, for your failure to become the ideal person you wanted to be. Such an indictment would be wrong and unjust. It would be wrong because it is self-pity. It would be unjust because it was not your parents alone who made you what you are at this moment. You yourself had a hand in that. So did your playmates, friends, neighborhood, teachers, and the time of history into which you happened to be born.

How would you like it if you knew that your own children, grown up, would blame you for what they are or failed to become?

Examine your parents' mistakes for a practical purpose—to learn, to be guided and directed by them. You are going to do better for your own children.

But look out; don't fool yourself. You are not going to be the perfect parent. You too are going to make mistakes.

You have a great advantage over your own parents, however—the advantage of a whole generation of increased knowledge, awareness, and understanding. And you have the yearning, the heartfelt desire and determination, to be the best possible parent. If you hadn't you would not be reading this.

So let's go back to the child who lives in each of us to explore the big question:

"If I were a child again this very minute, what would I want from my parents?"

You will probably go along with me in giving these answers:

I would want to know that my parents love me,

that they really want me, that they're glad I'm theirs, that I "belong."

I would want to know that they enjoy me, that they like playing and working with me, and that they know I am not a bad child but a good child who sometimes does things he shouldn't;

—that they take my feelings seriously even though I can't explain them and, for all their willingness and wisdom, they can't understand;

—that they are interested in my discoveries and experiences, and respect my developing ideas, notions, and opinions;

—that they feel I have something to contribute all of my own.

I would want to have as much family fun as possible, the wholesome and happy experience of doing all sorts of things together.

I would want my parents to guide me concurrently in all areas of my development—mental, physical, social, religious, and educational.

I would want to know that their discipline of me has rules, that the rules are firm but not rigid, and are really and truly meant to help me;

—that there is good sense behind each and every correction;

—that punishment is an extreme measure rarely applied, severe enough for its purposes but not terrorizing;

—that the rules are the same for my brothers and sisters;

—and that my parents themselves, in their grown-up

world, live by those very same rules, so that I can grow easily and naturally into the larger meaning of the rules: Justice, Fair Play, Truth, Consideration for Others, Responsibility, and Love.

Love and affection, respect, fun, guidance, and wise discipline are basic needs of all children, the guiding truth for parents who want to enjoy their children and who want their children to enjoy them, the world, and life.

For centuries the child was thought of as a miniature adult. From this point of view, if he did wrong it was evil—something deliberate which had to be whaled out of him. He had to learn through fear, misery, and heartbreak. We meet this unfortunate child again and again in the great stories of Charles Dickens, a writer who did not forget what it was like to be a child.

Yet, parents in all those centuries loved their children, and thought they were doing the right thing. They could not understand why, when they did so much for them, the children were not happy, loving, grateful, and good.

Perhaps it was these parents who, long ago, created the good fairy and the bad fairy. The good fairy made magic for the child, the bad fairy made magic against the child. So the child himself was not actually wicked; it all depended on which fairy happened to have the upper hand, or the stronger magic. That way, too, the parents didn't feel so guilty.

And perhaps it was these children, adult but remembering, who created stories in which they went out to slay ogres and dragons, trying to show their parents that they were Somebodies.

There is magic still in bringing up children—in fact, more than ever. It is a better magic than any conceived of by our bewildered ancestors, because it works. This magic does not come from any outside agency, but from within.

The other day, on my way home from a telecast, I passed a father and daughter walking along, completely absorbed in each other, the father stooping toward the small, upturned face. I overheard him say, ". . . and one mice is a mouse."

Instantly I was transported back into the enchantment of childhood, the wonder-world where things are new and astonishing, where more than one mouse is *mice* but more than one house does not want to become *hice*.

That father had entered into his little girl's world, and because of this would see his own in a fresh light. They would be growing up together, sharing the marvels. The magic works both ways: that's the great fun of it. The happy child does not go off all by himself into a fearful world to slay a dragon. He does the great deed at home, giving his parents ringside seats.

With this magic of love in your hearts, you and your child will have fun growing and learning together.

For many years parents have been writing me and telling me their problems. Although each child, each parent, and each problem is individually different, many of the questions boil down to the same thing.

I have seen how, through these years, my answers have changed, for it seems to me that I have grown with all the growing parents and children I have known. I am grateful to them. One is never finally grown up, but must always be growing. If grow one must, what happier way is there to grow than through and with parents and their children?

So it is out of gratitude that I sat down to get together the questions that recur most often, and to give the answers which have been broadening and deepening through the years. There are other parents who are asking these questions, or who are going to ask them, and I would like to help them, too. That is how this book came to be written, and why it is written in this way.

—Miss Frances

✻↯✤↯✻↯✤↯✻↯✤↯✻↯✤↯✺

ONE

In the beginning

✻↯✤↯✻↯✤↯✻↯✤↯✻↯✤↯✺

What shall I do?

Young Mrs. Smith rushed in and said, "I'm going to have a baby! What shall I do?"

"Be happy!" was my God-given reply.

She stared at me for a second, and then began to laugh. It was the most joyous laughter I had ever heard, and the most contagious. It was quite a while before we could settle down.

What were the troubles of Mr. and Mrs. Smith?

They didn't have any!

When they married they hoped to be blessed in time with a large family. They were a level-headed couple, and since they knew what they wanted they began, right after their honeymoon, to set aside every month a small sum of money "for baby." No emergency had required them to break into their precious fund. Now, two years later, they were ready.

Ideally ready. Mrs. Smith was in excellent physical condition. She and her husband loved each other more deeply than ever, now that they were going to be parents. And wisely they had seen to it that there were no financial worries.

What was the matter, then?

It was simply that ever since the doctor had told them the wonderful news they had been emotionally bowled over. Small disagreements became large. Simple practical matters became problems. "Let's be sensible," they kept telling each other. That very morning, when her husband had said it, the expectant mother burst into tears and threatened to go home to her mother.

When Mrs. Smith laughed, she was laughing, she confided, at herself. "Imagine!" she exclaimed. "We were remembering everything . . . and forgetting the most important thing—how happy we are!"

Some couples have more serious worries. Whatever they are, small or large, they are more easily confronted when husband and wife are sustained by a deep, serene happiness which is quite unshakable because they share the glory and look forward together. You have often seen such parents-to-be.

"What shall I do?" That question has been put to me in many ways and forms, but never so dramatically as that day by Mrs. Smith. Nor have I ever found a better answer: "Be happy!"

Where can we find out about new babies?

This question is one you should never hesitate to ask.

Your first source is your doctor, whose concern is, of course, your physical welfare. But he cannot spend hours and days with you, so it is good to know that there is a treasury of information within easy reach. Never has there been a civilization so fact-filled and helpful as ours for you and baby.

You can read books, magazines, and pamphlets. Some may be too scientific for you. Others may be too simple and lacking in the facts you really want. Or you may seek a touch of humor, philosophy, or religious inspiration with the facts. Not so long ago a list of recommended reading of this sort would have been quite short. Now such a list would be too long to be included here.

It can be fun to browse in bookstores and the library until you find just the thing that meets your individual need. Your doctor, friends, and the librarian may be of help in suggesting reading matter. You can also write to the Children's Bureau in Washington, D.C., for its publication, *Pre-Natal Care*, and at the same time ask for a list of the Bureau's publications on children. If you don't often get into town, it is heartening to know that this material is easily available, some of it free of charge.

There is another source of information: classes for future parents given by associations and organizations such as the Red Cross. Make inquiries about those in your community. Such classes can be invaluable not only for what you learn but also because they bring you into contact with other women preparing for motherhood. Usually it is best to attend these classes toward the end of your pregnancy—during the last two or three months. By the way, most of these classes are for expectant fathers as well as for mothers.

There is one source, however, from which you should accept advice with reservations. Before your baby is born you will have many conversations with your parents, friends, relatives, and neighbors—and most of them will give you free advice about how to handle the newcomer. Chances are you will be more confused than enlightened. You can be misinformed by those close to you, although their intentions are good and their interest sincere. *Always check with your doctor.*

We have to buy so many things. Where shall we begin?

If you are worried about this, it may reassure you to know that many other couples are, too.

If you feel a bit awkward or hesitant, start with the baby clothes. They are so adorable that as you go from store to store, you are likely to find yourself in a world of enchantment even before the baby arrives.

If you have a friend who has a young baby, she may be very helpful, particularly in making you aware of the difference between essentials and the extra things that are just nice to have. Remember that you may get some of these "extras" as gifts for the baby.

Most clerks in infant-wear departments or shops are eager to sell you what you will really need. Only rarely will one urge you to buy some luxury item when it is clear that you do not want or need it.

If you live far from town shops, you can purchase through mail-order catalogues just as you buy other things. Read carefully the description of each item, and get the catalogue of more than one company to make comparisons.

Go on from clothes to baby linen, pillow, blankets, and the like. You will probably be examining cribs and baby carriages at the same time. Both should be strong, for they will receive hard wear as baby grows older and more active.

Fortunately, carriages are neither as elaborate nor as bulky and cumbersome as they used to be. They are more functional and, because of the lightweight materials used in construction, can be more easily taken up and down steps, in and out of doorways, and so forth. Some are now so constructed that they can also serve as a bed on the back seat of an automobile. A good carriage, like a good crib, should be durable—strong enough to serve for your second baby, even for your third. When you make your purchase you should also have considered the size of the carriage in relation to where you will keep it.

Unless you have plenty of shelf and drawer space (and most of us don't these days) there must be a chest or wardrobe in which to keep the infant's clothing and linen. Examine the piece to make sure that it has enough room not only for now but also for later. See whether it permits you to get quickly and easily at what you want; you may want that something in a hurry. Try to make certain that the drawers, doors, or panels do not stick and that they don't make a lot of noise being opened and shut.

You will need the crib and a bathinet when you bring baby home, so these two items should be purchased before you go to the hospital. The bathinet should be comfortable and sturdy, without any sharp corners or rough spots. Naturally, its size is important, for it must fit into the space where you will be bathing the baby regularly. Today bathinets are so made that they can be folded and put out of sight when not in use; too, they may serve very well as the place on which to change the baby's diaper and other clothes.

The high chair is another piece of furniture that receives hard usage. When the baby is strong enough to sit up and to eat solid foods, he takes his meals there, and he is often seated there to play while Mother is busy nearby. The high chair must be sturdy and well balanced, because babies like to rock and pound and throw their weight about.

Two types of high chair are in general use. One is about dining-room-table height and has a tray for the food. The other is a self-contained, square table arrangement with the chair in the center, which gives the child the feeling of being seated at a table of his own. The legs and inside chair are adjustable so that you can raise them as baby grows. This type of high chair can be folded, almost like a card table, and is easy to travel with.

Shopping for baby is fun. Husbands are discovering this more and more, and taking part, so far as they can. Everything you do together, in the good feeling of wanting to share both joys and responsibilities, contributes that much more to love and understanding.

Should we buy the best of everything?

No, because the baby doesn't care. He wants only to be warm, clean, comfortable, and well looked after. If parents, by some special dispensation, were permitted to buy the stars out of the sky to adorn their babies tonight, the heavens would go starless!

Of course you want the best and loveliest of everything, and this is one time in your life when you may not find it easy to be satisfied with anything less. But right here is where you can begin to make the distinction between your own needs and those of your child. When you realize that it doesn't matter in the least to the baby, is it still so important to you to have the best of everything for him?

The distinction is difficult. You may feel that you want the beautiful and costly things because you love your baby so much. Yet the mere fact that these things are expensive cannot be appreciated by the tiny child and has nothing whatever to do with his health or happiness.

In later years the distinction between your own needs, desires, and tastes and those of your child is likely to be even harder for you to see. So why not begin to keep it in mind right now, when it is relatively clear and simple? It will help you in many ways, for it will become a basic consideration in countless decisions you will have to make as you grow up with your child.

Buy the expensive baby garments, bedclothes, furniture, and toys if you like them and can easily afford them. But don't make the mistake of thinking you are buying them *for your baby*. The baby, I repeat, doesn't care. And never forget that these lovely things, and your pride and pleasure in them, are no substitute for answering his real needs.

Here are some further considerations:

Even if you can afford to buy them, remember that the most expensive baby things are not necessarily best for the purpose.

Remember too that they will receive hard use and that the infant will soon outgrow them and need many more things.

Finally, never for a moment forget the most important thing for which money should always be available —baby's health and your own.

Keep in mind an ancient and simple adage—or write it down and place it where it will often catch your eye: "First things first."

What arrangements should I make before going to the hospital?

The last two months of pregnancy are the hardest. If you do not already have household help, now is the time to find a reliable girl or woman to come in and do the housework and the laundry once a week, or more often if you need her and can afford it.

You will want her to continue her work while you are in the hospital. See that she has a key so that she can come in while you are gone, for it will mean much to you to return to a clean, tidy home. It is not easy at any time to find the ideal maid or housekeeper, so do not expect or demand too much or you may find yourself without any help at all.

When you return home with the new member of the family, it is wonderful to have a practical nurse for a week or longer. She will help you over your first timidity in handling the baby. The practical nurse ideally takes over the household tasks as well, but here again do not expect the ideal, for nurses are in such great demand that only by keeping to "first things first"—in this case mother and baby—can you get along with the nurse. Therefore, it will be a good idea, if it is within your budget, to keep the maid on even if you have a nurse.

If yours is to be a bottle baby, you should have an infant nurse rather than a practical nurse. The infant nurse will take the night stretch and be up preparing the bottle and the formula and changing the baby while you get a good night's sleep, recovering your strength that much faster. If you intend to breast-feed your baby you'll have to get up anyway, and you will not need a night nurse.

Your doctor arranges for the hospitalization—you have only to say whether you want private, semiprivate, or ward accommodation. As your time nears you should have arranged for transportation, and will need to have a small suitcase packed and at hand, containing two or three shortie nightgowns, toilet articles, a robe, and similar items. Have a second small bag ready with baby's things—about three diapers, the tiny undershirt, a little dress, blankets to wrap him in or a bunting if the weather is cold. Your husband or a relative can bring this the day before you and baby go home; at that time you can also arrange for transportation home.

Diaper services are now almost universal—and what a blessing they are! This too should be arranged for in advance of hospitalization. The usual order is for 80–100 a week for two months. Many mothers retain the convenient service for a third month, some for as long as a year or more.

You know that you will have to get up sometime, perhaps many times, for baby during the night, so think about a night light. If you start up and snap on the ordinary light, its brightness will give you some dazed, blinking moments. It will also wake your husband. There are small night-globes of about ten watts which can be kept burning all night. Some prefer to snap on a soft-glow, well-shaded bedlamp. One mother found her best solution was a pencil-size flashlight she kept under her pillow.

If husband and wife have prepared well emotionally, there is no need for me to remind the expectant mother of one "arrangement" which cannot be made like the others. It is, rather, a basic attitude—its foundation, love and considerateness. In the course of your tremendous, overwhelming experience of becoming a mother, don't forget or ignore your husband!

How can we name our baby to please everyone?

You can't, nor should you try. This question usually indicates that you have relatives, with strong opinions on the matter, with whom you disagree. If there is a name which has been passed on from generation to generation in either family, why not make it the baby's middle name? Family tradition is precious, after all, and should not be thoughtlessly tossed away.

Your first and foremost consideration is, of course, your baby—the individual who is going to carry for life the name you select. Interesting psychological studies have been made on the subject of names. One thing they reveal is that, by and large, girls wear the fancier names better than boys do. Boys prefer the more standard names. Your public library is sure to have at least one book on naming the baby, listing hundreds of names with derivation and meaning.

The first name should go euphonically with the surname. It should lend itself to an attractive nickname, or at least not lend itself to an unattractive one which may later embarrass the child or cause him to be teased by his schoolmates.

Say the complete name aloud. Try it for sound.

Take your time. Selecting the name is an absorbing part of parenthood and should be thoroughly enjoyed.

Whatever name is finally decided upon, it should have the agreement of both parents.

Is our baby as helpless and fragile as he looks?

The first few times, most mothers are a little nervous about handling a baby. This is quite natural. You have only to look at the baby to realize how helpless he is. You take him up, and the little head wobbles; he is so tiny that your arms, which you had somehow thought would be filled, seem to have hardly anything to hold.

Then, suddenly, you feel the amazing strength in the small hands and the mouth. And if he is being mishandled, you hear him!

These first signs that baby does have strength, and can—in his limited way—let you know how you are doing, are so relieving and reassuring that many mothers forget their fears almost at once. After the first week the routine activities of feeding, bathing, and diapering come more easily and with enjoyment.

Yes, baby *is* as helpless as he looks in the sense that he cannot do anything for himself and is wholly dependent upon you. But he is not as fragile as he may seem.

There is really no need to be afraid of doing things for your baby. Only remember that sure and gentle handling gives him security.

Are all babies dictators?

Young Mrs. Brown was recalling her life before little Kathy's arrival—preparing her husband's favorite dishes, sitting down to her favorite television programs, having time for shopping and the beauty salon, entertaining at home or going out with her husband, sleeping late on week-end mornings. . . . "Everything is so different now," she said. "A new baby is a dictator. Are they all like that?"

She was not complaining, only wondering. She and her husband had known it would be this way, but there are different kinds of knowing. It is one thing to see a situation from afar and quite another to be right in it.

As soon as baby comes home, your routine is remade to revolve round his feeding and sleeping schedule. Everything else has to take second place. In that sense your baby is a dictator. You are not complaining, but sometimes, particularly after a hard day and night, you think back, a little wistfully. . . .

When you do, it is because you are very tired. Keeping your baby comfortable, your husband in good spirits, your home attractive, and your table appetizing takes management and work. But you must also take care of yourself, physically, emotionally, and socially. You can best help your baby if you are strong and happy and confident.

As soon as you feel that you may safely leave your baby for a few hours in someone's care—grandmother, aunt, or a reliable sitter—go out with your husband in the evening, and occasionally with your friends in the afternoon. Getting away, even if it's only for an hour or two, is refreshing and strengthening.

Going out is also good for your husband. He loves the baby too, but to come home night after night to an exhausted wife who has no time for him and whose physical and emotional state fills him with helpless anxiety—well, you know how he feels.

To go back to the direct question: "Are all babies dictators?"

Yes. Their dictates are not whims or crankiness. They are life-needs and cannot be neglected. But these needs are actually quite simple, and once you settle down to the routine imposed by your baby's schedule, you will have little difficulty and much pleasure in being a mother, a wife, and a housekeeper all at the same time.

Why does baby cry?

Because it is the only way he can let you know he is unhappy and needs you. In the beginning his crying means "I'm hungry" or "I'm wet and want to be changed." Or both. Of these two needs hunger is the more urgent. Don't wake baby up just to change him; he needs his sleep much more than you need yours. (By the way, it has been discovered that baby girls are more likely to fuss about being wet than boys.)

Baby will cry, of course, if he is in pain or is frightened. He may also cry if he is lonely, for at the bottom of loneliness is fear of some kind.

"I think babies are born with built-in crying machinery," one mother remarked to me.

This is true. The smile comes later and is imitative —it is a response to and imitation of your own smile. And it is as baby grows that he develops the happy chuckle which is the most delightful sound ever made, and which develops, in turn, into laughter.

Is there more than one kind of cry?

There certainly is. When your baby is suffering pain or discomfort he makes a different sound from, for example, his cry of loneliness. When he has had a shock of pain or fright there is rage in the cry. Soon you learn to distinguish one kind of cry from another.

There is a note of helplessness in all of a baby's crying. When he is left to "cry himself out," a note of hopelessness enters. To my mind this is the most desolate sound in the world. It means that an infant just starting out in life is being given to understand that he cannot get help when he wants it. Not even mature adults can accept this kind of dismal lesson philosophically, even though we all do have to swallow it now and then.

Why are babies afraid of unfamiliar people?

I recall a grandmother who was deeply hurt because her infant grandchild cried whenever she approached. It took her some time to become aware of what she was doing. She would rush at the baby, swoop down, and go into ecstatic exclamations. He was frightened.

Uncle Bill has a heavy step, a hearty voice, and a cigar. He walks up to baby's crib and booms, full of pride and love, "And how's my big, beautiful girl today?" His big, beautiful girl gives him a wide stare, pulls back, and cries.

It doesn't always happen, but it happens more often than not. As in their reactions to their parents, babies are sensitive to the behavior of others. Swift motion, sudden and extreme gestures, loud voices, and grown-up excitement frighten them until they learn by experience that there is no threat to them in all the commotion.

I remember a family gathering in the course of which everyone at the same time became aware of the spectacular sunset outside. They rushed to the windows, flung them open, and cried out to one another, "Look! Just look! Isn't it gorgeous!" In the midst of this pleasurable excitement, year-old Robert began to cry. No one needed to be told that he was frightened by the grown-ups' sudden burst of noise and activity. While Bobby was taken aside by his mother to be soothed and reassured, the adults proceeded to enjoy nature on a quieter note.

Often relatives or friends want to hold the baby. If he squirms or cries, he is being held in a way uncomfortable to him.

When the baby is afraid of someone, it is no personal reflection on that individual. It may not be easy to persuade the offended adult of this. But it is even harder to explain to the infant that grandmother, Uncle Bill, or whoever, means no harm. It is up to the adult to understand what the infant can only learn in time.

Little by little the parents, acting as shield and liaison, can bring baby and the other grownups together.

What does a baby really understand?

One mother told me: "I talk to my little Mary about everything and anything—you know, like what I'm making for Daddy's supper, and the weather, and what her

Aunt Jane just said on the phone, and the new curtains I'm sewing. My neighbor thinks I'm crazy, but I don't care. We have fun!"

Mary was only two months old and certainly couldn't understand what her mother was saying. But she did know enough to gurgle and kick happily. She was learning very early that communication is pleasant and that she was part of the family. That mother was wise. She was enjoying her baby, and she knew that little Mary was, in her own way, enjoying and getting to know Mother.

What does a baby *really* understand?

Both more and less than we can know or imagine.

The infant is new to the world and he is being bombarded with impressions: heat, cold, light, sound, movement. Each of the impressions is important insofar as it does something to and for him. Groups and repetitions of impressions pile up within the tiny being who quickly knows and registers this much: They are pleasant or unpleasant, pro or con. This is the beginning of all learning.

At the same time the mother and father are getting acquainted with their baby, he is becoming acquainted with them and with a broadening world of experiences. Gradually he learns to recognize their touch, their voices, and the many things they do with and for him every day, and to associate them with the pleasant feelings.

Your baby is growing. While he is accumulating, registering, and sorting out experiences, he is also getting to know and use his body more and more. One day when you are smiling down at him, a muscle twitches in your baby's face, smooths, twitches again—holds. He is smiling right back at you!

Can you ever forget the magic of that moment? As a matter of fact, you can and do, because so much else comes along. That is why many parents like to keep a baby diary, an album of photographs, movies, and tape recordings. I well recall the awe in a young father's voice when he told me that his baby daughter had turned over all by herself for the first time. She was only three weeks old. He was overjoyed and **very proud**, and had to tell everyone about it.

Each baby learns—stores and registers his experiences and responds to them—at his own individual pace. He knows when he is unhappy, and he cries. He knows when he is having fun with you, and he smiles. Growing, he becomes active, and quite soon he knows when you say "No!" and mean it, and when you don't mean it.

It is then that the question of what baby really understands becomes of major importance. Because now he does *really* understand, better than you perhaps know.

Can we spoil our baby by too much attention?

Not when attention is accompanied by consideration. For example, you are playing with your baby and have been having a wonderful time, and so has he. Quite suddenly he begins to cry. A second ago he was smiling. He began to cry almost tentatively, as if trying it out, and now he goes on and on, crying bitterly. Some parents, stopped like this in the middle of their own fun, feel disappointment.

What has probably happened is that there has been too much petting, stroking, handling, kissing, tickling, cooing. He has become irritated or overexcited, or you may actually have hurt him by playing a bit too roughly. Whatever it was, it was a little more playing than he could take.

Overstimulation arouses strong sensations of pleasure, of the kind that verge on the unpleasant. If such incidents continue, the baby may develop a craving for the strong sensations even though they end in tears and fretting—and you find yourself with a cranky baby. So you can see that when he becomes "spoiled," it is not always because of love.

Sometimes it may be hard for you to realize that you are going too far. Baby's skin is so soft and satiny, and his body such a joy to fondle, that in your enjoyment you may easily forget how quickly he tires; and also how quickly, for him, pain and pleasure may become confused.

I know parents who say in such cases, "I'm so sorry!" as they quickly prepare baby for bed.

Apologizing to a baby?

Yes, and I admire them for it.

How can we know if we are doing the right things?

If your baby is happy, you are doing fine. I don't mean happy every minute of the day, of course. Nor do I mean to say that a happy baby never cries. But if he smiles, talks to himself as well as to you, experiments with the things around him, eats and sleeps well, you can be pretty sure that you have a happy baby.

See to it that you and your husband spend some time each day with the baby, not only in taking care of his basic needs but also in playing (within the baby's limits), singing, talking. Babies should not always be isolated in their cribs and play pens. They should begin their social development with the family the day they are brought home from the hospital.

Have your baby checked regularly by your pediatrician. You want to be sure, always, that he is physically well and growing stronger as well as bigger.

✲✦❀✦✦❀✦✲✦❀✦✲✦❀✦✲❀✦❀

TWO

Suddenly a child

✲✦❀✦✲✦❀✦✲✦❀✦✲✦❀✦✲✦❀

When does our baby become a child?

In general, children under one year of age are referred to as infants or babies, but there is no fixed rule. There is no line which a baby crosses to become, magically, a child, leaving babyhood behind forever.

Infancy is the stage of helpless dependence. It does not last long. Even in infancy the little one is observing and responding, digesting experiences as well as food, reaching, and trying things out. He is growing not only in size and strength, but in all ways. The life-forces within him make him strive to stand on his own feet and to express himself—to become an individual who can do things for himself.

Parents want to see their baby grow, and would be

28

much alarmed if he did not. Yet, in a way, they hate to see him grow up. These two very human but opposing emotions may clash. Some parents try to keep their child babyish, dependent—while at the same time they say, when the child annoys them, "Don't do that. You're a big boy (or girl) now!"

The result of this mixed attitude is confusion, to say the least. And emotional confusion is not a healthful climate for anyone, child or grownup.

As soon as you hear your child say a word or two that can be clearly understood (by others as well as yourself) as something he intended to say, be prepared. He is leaving babyhood. His mind and his body co-ordinated to bring out the words—to communicate. From now on, mind and body will work more and more together. The marvelous and tremendously complicated thinking process has begun.

How can we help him walk and talk?

This question is one all parents should consider when their little one is stepping from babyhood into childhood.

The baby is carried from one place to another. The very young child, while he still likes and needs to be carried, wants more and more to get around by himself. And he certainly does move about!

As he becomes more active and sure, his speed increases surprisingly. So does the range of his excursions.

He goes from one room to another, and is suddenly underfoot. How in the world does he get around so fast?

At this time you have to work out plans to keep him away from dangerous areas, such as stairs, swinging doors, the stove, electric outlets, and the like. Nor will you have dangling cloths which he can pull to bring things down on his head—nor will you have matches within his reach.

The crawler–toddler is a great explorer. He is beginning to see the world from a different angle. He will start picking up objects and putting them into his mouth to get to know them that way. He will soon be taking things out of containers, such as sewing and wastebaskets. He is going to discover that he can bang one object on another, such as a spoon on a pot, and make a marvelous racket. This gives him a sense of power as well as joy.

You are going to say "No!" a lot, and must take things away from him—firmly but not angrily. Very soon you see him hesitate and look up at you when he is about to do something to which "No" has been attached. It is a great moment, even though he may go through with the action anyway.

When the child sets out on one of his excursions, he seems to be saying to everyone in the family, "Here I come, get everything out of my way!" Of course you can't possibly get everything out of his way. He is going to bump into things, fall, and have other accidents.

He can take a lot of bumps and bruises, so you should not make a fuss over him when he does bang himself. It is the fuss rather than the hurt that often sets a child crying—if no to-do is made he often picks himself up and starts off again. If you do make a fuss, he may not only start crying but later may take a fall deliberately because of the excitement it arouses and the attention it brings him. Or he may become frightened and overcautious so that his natural adventurousness and the development it brings will be hindered. Make sure the hurt is not serious if you're in any doubt, but treat the accident casually, as if it were all part of the game. (Your pediatrician can tell you what first-aid remedies to keep on hand.)

The child is actually looking to you for guidance on the emotional and physical gravity of what he has done or what has happened to him. His shock or pain is rarely so great that he can't get over it quite easily. But you make it hard for him to get over it by an over-solicitous attitude.

Sympathy and concern are good, but don't continue them too long. Here is one place where you may sense your child trying you out. He may try to see how much attention he can get. There need be no difficulty. He can easily be distracted.

Now that he is toddling, you have to start thinking about buying him shoes. Consult your pediatrician about this, and particularly about the kind of shoes to buy. A child's feet need good support and complete comfort. The wrong shoes can retard his desire to walk as well as damage his feet.

With talking there is an entirely different problem, one of which some parents are unaware.

The child's first clear words should sound an alert to the parents, reminding and warning them that children build vocabularies from the words they hear spoken around them. Are you using words you wouldn't want your child to use?

How and why the child picks out what he does remains a mystery. Once he begins, he picks up a great deal and often surprises you. Some words, big and small, give him special pleasure. Whether it is the fun of rolling them on the tongue, or the sound in itself as it falls on his ear, we are not sure, but he does like to say them over and over again. Often he laughs when he says them. They tickle his fancy in some way.

A child uses words freely long before he knows their full meaning. For the most part he is only making sounds he has heard, which he finds himself at last able to utter, and which, when he says them, bring smiles, praise, encouragement.

Speech is imitative.

Suppose you are using "darn it!" in your everyday vocabulary. One day your child suddenly says "oh, darn it" in very much your own manner. You can't help laughing, and indeed it is funny. So the child will be saying it again, proudly.

I know a couple who found themselves with a serious problem. The father, from long service in the army, had brought back a barracks vocabulary which he continued to use freely. He was hugely amused when little Michael began to say the words. One summer day when he and his wife and child were out for a walk, they stopped at a traffic light. The occupants of a car that drew up beside them admired the beautiful little boy and began to talk to him. From the little mouth issued a stream of words that made them freeze with horror. Michael's mother made a firm decision. She told her husband in terse but unprofane language that he must mend his ways. He did, but it was not easy to undo the damage. In fact, it took years.

What I mean is that if you do not want your child to use bad language, don't use it yourself. Then, if the child brings in a "naughty" word he has learned outside, you will be able to explain that there are certain words which are not polite, that you yourself do not say them, and that you do not think he will want to say them either.

You have, in effect, set a family standard and are in a good position to impose that standard on your child.

Let me end this with two cautions about the child's first words and first steps.

One: Grownups should control their emotion. Screams of delight or pride can easily frighten the small child into not trying again for a long time.

Two: Do not try to make your child repeat again and again what he has done or said. He has fully enjoyed the doing or saying, and your praise and approval along with it, and will repeat of his own accord. He should not be pushed. Being asked to show off, when he is not ready or has no desire to do so, is extremely irritating for anyone, adult or child. It is especially so for younger children.

These two cautions are difficult to exercise. All the same, consider that your child's development is at stake. You do not want to put any emotional blocks in his way.

How can we get our son to eat what he should?

You may be pushing him. It is in feeding that you are most likely to become demanding and impatient, and to exert pressure. But overconcern often results in the child's dawdling over his meal or developing a number of food dislikes.

I have often wondered what it would be like if I were eighteen months or two years old and my mother bore down upon me grimly every morning with a poached egg, and a spoon which in her determined hands became a weapon!

The harder you try to make your child eat, the more resistance he displays. Don't let feeding become a major crisis. One cannot start too early to establish good eating habits. Avoid the attitude that unless he eats what you want him to, you will feed it to him forcibly.

Many a mother standing over her rebellious child cries out, "But you've got to! It's good for you!"

Is she as right as she is righteous?

Well, let's see. Go back to the tiny baby. Suppose your baby at one time or another rejects his bottle. Do you get cross with him?

No. You try to find the source of the trouble. The formula may have been changed a little too radically for him, or the temperature isn't right. Or the baby may be emotionally upset because of too much play and handling —or because you yourself are upset for some reason; your baby is highly sensitive to your moods. Or he may not want to eat simply because he is not hungry.

You do not force your baby to eat, because you know very well it would not be good for him. A child should not be forced either, and for exactly the same reason. Eating is, and always should be, a pleasure.

When you begin to change the diet to include more solid food, your child may at first reject it completely. If this happens, it is wise to assume he is not ready for it. He may, however, take it tentatively and accept only a very little. In that case you can try it again quite soon, where in the first case you would wait a little longer. The child has to get used to the new taste and consistency and decide for himself that he likes it. You should not offer the new food in haste, tension, or anxiety.

If a child refuses essential food too consistently, or is fretful when taking it, there is still another factor to be considered. His weaning often coincides with teething, which may be quite painful. It is therefore all the more important to be soothing and comforting at feeding time.

Offer the new formula or the new food as something pleasant. If the child clearly refuses it, accept this rejection quietly and casually. If there is too much rejection, so that you become worried about his health, don't worry the child with your worry. Consult your pediatrician instead.

A mother who tries to force food in, telling her child he's got to eat "because mother won't love you if you don't," or "because mother knows best," or "because it's good for you," is initiating a strained relationship between herself and her child.

There may be times when the child must take something that is *really* for his own good—on the doctor's instructions. In that case you should both explain and sympathize. The very young child may not understand the explanation but he will understand the sympathy, and will thus be more easily comforted when the unpleasantness is over.

It was not too long ago that little or no attention was paid to children's feelings when it came to medication. You may not remember back to the days when children were dosed with a huge tablespoonful of liquid, raw, straight-from-the-fish cod-liver oil. It was good for us, of course. But whenever I remember, I shudder!

Nowadays, medication of any kind for infants and

children is carefully prescribed and has been prepared to give a minimum of disagreeable taste or reaction.

What kind of game is our child playing when he throws things? Should we always pick them up for him?

Mrs. Carter, mother of three, put it this way:

"It does seem to me that little children, even babies, play games with their parents. Why, for instance, does my youngest, sitting in his high chair, drop his spoon or a toy over the side, and then look at me as if to say, 'Please pick that up'? When I hand it back to him, he throws it again, and when I ignore him cries for me to pick it up. I'd be retrieving for him all day long if he had his way. Why do the little rascals do it?"

Mrs. Martin said, "I think the little rascals have found out that they have power over us grownups. I stopped mine right away. I won't have my children bossing me!"

Mrs. Carter was more tolerant and understanding of her children's ways, but she shared Mrs. Martin's point of view—that the child's dropping-throwing games become deliberate after the first few successful times.

Both my visitors were keen observers of their children, so as we talked it over we learned a good deal. We considered the first times a child drops or throws an object. Do you remember the pause that followed? It was something like what you yourself do when you hear a crash. For a second or two you hold stock-still, your whole being registering. And from the stillness emerges the question, "What happened?"

Of course the little child doesn't react to the same things you do or in the same way. But certain responses are fundamentally the same, since they begin in early childhood. What has happened for the child who drops or throws something?

He was having fun waving and banging his rattle. He was not aware that the muscles of his hand were contracted from holding the object, and would quickly tire. When they did tire they sent through him the motor impulse to release. Result: He drops the rattle, or gets rid of it by throwing.

The child does not know clearly that he has done something. He only knows that something has happened. What he knows is that he was having a grand time with the rattle or a spoon, and suddenly it's gone! The pause is a surprised one. The child seems to be registering the fact that his plaything has disappeared.

The first time this occurs, and perhaps the second and third times as well, this seemingly trivial incident is quite a big event to the child. He turns to the nearest grownup for help. His look carries appeal and distress. That is why you respond just as if you had been ordered to. You respond automatically to a clear appeal for help. You pick up rattle or spoon and restore it to him.

The child keeps on dropping or throwing and you

continue to respond. It takes only a little time before he learns that he himself has done something, that the toy hasn't disappeared forever, and that if he wants to keep it he must not let it drop. That's a lot to learn. It really means learning the laws of cause and effect.

But a complication is that the child sometimes throws things, food even, in refusal of them. It's a natural gesture—"Away with it!"

There are, then, two different actions of dropping or throwing things. One becomes playful. This is not intended to make Mother pick up after him. His muscular impulses impel him to do this; he finds pleasure in it and has no idea that it might annoy anyone.

In the rejection by means of getting rid of an unwanted thing, the same muscular work appears but without the pleasure. The gesture is one of dislike, even of anger. He does *not* want that thing back.

What happens, it seems to me—and Mrs. Martin and Mrs. Carter agreed—is not just that Mother gets tired of picking up. She confuses the play-throwing with the away-with-it act. The child's forceful rejection betrays elements of anger and rebellion. These emotions are highly contagious. Even from one little son or daughter they are catching. Mother becomes irritated before she realizes it. And she doesn't realize, until she analyzes, that it is the rejection-throwing (and the anger it arouses in her) that makes a mother feel her children are playing a game with her.

I have spent a lot of time on this subject because it helps us to understand so much.

We see that a child's activities in his first years are directed primarily by his muscular impulses.

We see that two actions that appear alike are not necessarily alike—in the child any more than in the grownup.

We see that playfulness is one thing and rejection quite another, not only in themselves but in the emotions they arouse in others.

We see that grownups do, sometimes in spite of their best endeavors, respond strongly to a child's "anti" emotions. And that the equally emotional response makes them feel they are being used, ordered about, more or less deliberately, by the child. This feeling, so natural and human, is mistaken.

Now, to return to the question posed some time back—to pick up or not to pick up the playfully discarded toy?

Yes, you should pick it up, and you will, for some time. When you tire of playing baby's game, try distracting him into doing something else. This is far easier than trying to stop him by saying "No!" A child confined to high chair or play pen hasn't much choice of activity. He can't retrieve the object himself. The throwing–dropping game is a signal to think about giving him more play space. When he is on the floor with lots of room to get around in, he can pursue his own tosses and will learn more quickly about cause and effect.

The prescription for the rejection kind of throwing is something else again. It calls for teaching in good social behavior.

Why won't our child do this week what he was doing perfectly well last week?

Some parents are quite upset when a child who was beginning to feed himself, dress or undress, respond to "No," or go to the toilet regularly, reverts suddenly to his former helplessness in one activity or another. They scold him, and he shrinks back, cries, or just stares and maybe sucks his thumb.

A child does not learn something completely, once and for all. But does anyone? Trial and error is the usual process.

A growing child often develops vague fears. He will then go back to baby ways in the unconscious search for security. At such times particularly, patience and love are required on the part of parents. It is usually difficult to find out what may be troubling a small child. You may, in fact, not discover it for a long time. But you can't go wrong if, at this time, you pay him more attention, spend a little more time with him than you have been doing.

For example, a child is sucking his thumb. Mother says, "Darling, you know you shouldn't do that," and firmly brings his hand down. He stares at her—and then, automatically, the hand rises; back goes thumb into mouth. Mother pulls it out again. They stare at each other, mother and child. The mother thinks she has won and goes about her tasks. When she glances at the child again, his thumb is in his mouth.

A child may be sucking his thumb or reverting in other ways to babyhood, for years. He is in some way comforting himself through this activity, and the question to be asked and answered is "What is troubling him?"

Does this mean we should let our child do anything he wants?

No. The small child looks to you for guidance and direction. Your concern is to guide and direct the very best you can. A petulant or sullen child isn't much fun for his parents. He isn't any fun for himself, either. Everything is easier when he is happy. A child who is not guided and directed will feel lost, unprotected; he will be chronically unhappy.

I will go into this subject more fully later in Chapter Five, "We guide our child."

Our two-year-old pokes his fingers in the electric outlets. How can we deter him?

Two-year-olds wander all around the house not only looking at everything within their reach but also poking and pulling to see how each thing works.

Your heart skips a beat when you see your child experiment with the electric outlets which he can reach so easily. First he usually pulls out the lamp cord and then he tries to put his finger into one of the narrow holes. When he finds that his fingers don't fit into the holes, he looks around for something else he can push in —silverware, for example. Obviously, this can be very dangerous.

When your child starts for the electric outlet the first time, explain to him that he cannot do this because these outlets are not to be played with. Be firm but not cross, and send him off to do something else.

The next time he heads toward the outlet, stop him and then remind him that he is not to touch it. Again explain why. Then try to interest him in one of his toys or books.

The third time this happens, and there will be a third and maybe a fourth time, stop him again, but this time isolate him on a chair or somewhere away from the outlet. Then explain to him that this will happen each time until he can remember not to go near the electric outlet. Keep him on the chair for five or ten minutes, and when he gets up remind him why he had to sit on the chair.

Take a look around your house or apartment and see what other dangerous things there are which could cause your young child to have a serious accident. Apply preventative measures. Some parents, for example, cover electric outlets that are not in use with adhesive or friction tape.

Are all matches high beyond his reach? This should also be true of sharp-pointed scissors, boxes of pins and needles, and sharp knives.

When you cook are the handles of your pots and pans turned in so that when your child walks past the kitchen range he can't grab or accidentally overturn them? This can keep him from getting badly burned.

It is necessary to keep temptation away from the young child who is not tall enough to see what is on the top of tables. When he can't see what is there he wants either to climb up and find out or pull the table over to him, and then everything comes tumbling down. This is especially true when he pulls a tablecloth.

Our child is growing so fast that clothing him has become a real expense. Should we buy clothes that he can grow into?

If the child's clothes are too big for him they slide down, trip him up, or are generally uncomfortable. They make him feel unconfident and may hold him back in his physical activities so that you find him doing more sitting and less climbing and running.

Children do outgrow their clothes at a fast rate, often before they wear them out. Many parents get together to swap or pass on their children's clothes. In this way the children continue to have comfortable clothes at reduced expense. When there is more than one child in the family, "hand-me-downs" serve the same purpose.

If or when the child who receives a "hand-me-down" objects, and the clothes do fit him comfortably, it is likely that he is becoming style-conscious. Styles do change, even in children's clothing, and a child likes to wear what the other children are wearing—not so much for style in the adult sense as to be a fully accepted member of his group.

How can we prepare our child for his first haircut?

There is still another new experience awaiting you and your young child. This is his first haircut.

For the child a haircut is important because he will no longer have to answer questions as to whether he is a boy or girl. For his mother a child's first haircut is a trying experience because she hates to see the baby curls go. The father is filled with pride because it is usually he who takes his son to the barber. This is real evidence of the father–son relationship. He is happy about it—provided all goes well at the barber shop.

The big event with the barber will go well, if some important things have happened before the eventful day. These aren't many, but they are essential.

A week or so before his first haircut, take a walk with your child in the direction of the barber shop and pause at the shop for a while to show him the large chairs and the men alongside them in their white uniforms. Talk with him about haircutting in general.

All conversation about the forthcoming haircut should be pleasant. Emphasize that the barber uses the scissors very carefully. Avoid threats of what will happen if your child doesn't sit still. Talk about the small seat that will be placed in the big chair; likewise, about the big apron that he will wear.

Be sure that you select a barber who not only has had experience in cutting children's hair, but who also enjoys children. If he is friendly and affectionate with your child, there is not apt to be a problem. Children can sense immediately whether the barber really likes them.

The first haircut is an indication to the child that he is now a "big boy." If it is a happy experience, he returns home with a smile and a "big-boy walk." Daddy is fully convinced that he and his son are pals and Mother looks and sees that the curls are gone, but she, too, is proud of her big boy.

What qualifications should we look for in a baby sitter?

When you are away, who is taking care of your child? All too often parents answer this question with "Whoever we've been able to get."

A mother and father told me of a frightening experience they will never forget. They had been invited out to dinner and their regular sitter notified them she couldn't come. On recommendation of their neighbors they managed to get a fifteen-year-old girl who had sat many times with other youngsters in the community. Their daughter was two. They gave Elizabeth, the new baby sitter, careful instructions.

At 12:30 the parents returned. Entering the house, they smelled smoke. They raced upstairs. Their child was sound asleep but her bedside lamp was on and was smoking and they had come just in time to keep the lampshade from bursting into flame.

When the father went downstairs to look for Elizabeth he found her sitting in his den, completely absorbed in the blaring television. "Oh, hello," she called. "I didn't hear you come in."

While he drove her home, the father described the tragedy that would have occurred if they had returned only minutes later. He advised her not to sit again with children until she clearly understood the responsibility of her job.

A reliable baby sitter must have certain basic qualifications:

1. She must be honest. This is not limited to merely "not taking things." She must be able to tell you the truth about herself and about what took place while you were away.

2. She must be able to understand and follow directions. It is always a good idea to write out directions clearly. Then let her read them back to you.

3. She must be able to use good judgment. If the child begins to cry and will not be comforted, she must know that she should phone you and ask for further directions. (Always leave with her a telephone number at which you can be reached, and the numbers of at least two of your neighbors and the doctor.) She must also know that the door is not to be opened to strangers, and that she cannot bring in her friends unless you know them and give permission.

4. A sitter must understand that she is there to take care of your child. She may entertain herself only insofar as it does not make her forget her job.

5. A baby sitter must like children. You must make sure that she is not merely pretending to like them, to get the job.

6. Parents must feel confidence in the sitter. With a new one they will always be a little worried. Confidence and trust can grow only with time and experience.

Girls ranging in age from twelve to eighteen are the most popular baby sitters. Be sure that, regardless of her years, your sitter is sufficiently mature to understand and assume her responsibilities. Sometimes a girl of eighteen is not as mature as one of twelve in this respect. You cannot automatically assume that a girl, or even a grown woman, is a responsible person merely because of age.

Sometimes relatives like to sit with your child. This can work well, provided they have the qualifications listed above.

The right kind of boy can also make a good sitter.

In all this I have been talking about the baby sitter and you. How about baby sitter and the child?

It is important to prepare your child for the sitter, as much as you can. He should be "introduced" to the sitter, just as he is presented to other grownups; you should watch them together for some time before you leave.

Further, tell your child that you are going out, and when you expect to return. Get into this habit from the start, even though it may seem a little silly. Habit is important. If you don't begin early, later you will be walking out and letting the child find out by himself that you are gone. This may be a terrible experience for him.

This tiny baby whom you have brought home from the hospital has grown from infancy to early childhood. He talks and walks; he plays and works hard at things; he runs and falls, but he keeps right on trying. He has had his first haircut, worn out several pairs of shoes, and also has outgrown his snowsuit, his crib, and his play pen. He is no longer a baby. He is convinced that he is a big boy . . . because you have told him that these things would happen when he grew up to be a big boy.

Yet, at the age of two, three, or even four, in your eyes your child is still a small boy. You will remember to respect him as a "big boy," won't you?

❋⚘❋⚘❋⚘❋⚘❋⚘❋⚘

The magic of toys, play, and television

❋⚘❋⚘❋⚘❋⚘❋⚘❋⚘

What toys can we buy that our child will be sure to enjoy?

Wooden building blocks, stuffed animals, trucks, picture puzzles, and dolls are used and enjoyed by children for years because they offer wide scope for imagination. The toddler likes a pull-toy. The usual development is from the pull-toy to the small wagon that he can fill with blocks or other small toys and pull to "deliver" from one place to another. On the beach or in the sand-pile the little shovel or scoop and pail fill the same pur-pose. You see him busy filling up, lugging the load a few feet, emptying it, and going back for a refill. Later he is delighted to be pulled by Daddy or Mother in the wagon. And when he shares the wagon with a playmate, pulling his little friend in it or being pulled in turn (although they may quarrel over who is to ride and who to pull), they are both learning the rules and fun of fair play and taking turns—sociability.

The ball is another basic toy. It becomes an important part of the growing child's life, especially when he begins to play with other children, so he should have one early. Ballplaying is largely social. That is, you must participate in it with the child, rolling the ball to him, trying to get him to roll it back to you. Then he learns to throw the ball into a box or basket, which helps him coordinate his arm muscles and judge space. Later you show him that it can be bounced and caught. His interest grows with his ability to use and control the ball.

Through play materials or toys a child learns a great deal about the everyday activities in the family, and in the community. He uses them as a way of trying out the things that he sees. For example, children like to play doctor, because this has been a part of their experiences since infancy. They use whatever play materials they have to carry out the many different things they have seen the doctor do when they visited him in his office, or when he came to see them at home.

Girls use their dolls and doll dishes again and again in the ways they see their mothers use them, setting the table and serving the dinner. Not only does this give them the experience of setting the table, it also gives them a chance to try out many different ways of playing hostess to their doll guests. They relive incidents they have seen take place in their family activities.

Can a child have too many toys?

Yes. A child can have too many toys, exclusive of records, books, and creative materials like crayons and paints, which I do not include in the category of toys.

The child who has too many toys has that much less opportunity to use his imagination, to pretend; less urge to be resourceful, to invent or make things. He does not see the play possibilities of each toy. For example, if your child owns an all-purpose truck, a dump truck, and a mail truck, he doesn't have the fun of using the one big truck for everything he can think of and act out. He is less inclined to play the all-important game of pretend. It is far better for a child to invent his own play and games and build his own castles—sand, block, or otherwise—than to be furnished with chests full of store-bought gadgets.

Imagination is not a part of the body you can see or locate. But it is very much a part of the growing mind and personality, and it is magically creative when encouraged or even given a chance. By use of his imagination the child will act out many things—wishes and yearnings, his version of the life around him, and even problems, inner troubles you may not know he has. Child psychologists and teachers have discovered, in fact, that the dramatic games a child plays when given a set of puppets, a variety of dolls, and building blocks furnish clues to the way his mind is running.

When a child does not have too many toys, he is likely to use them more, to be fonder of them, and to discover more play possibilities in each of them than you could have thought possible.

Why is a child so careless with his toys?

First of all, take a good look at his toys. Are they the kind that break or come apart easily?

A toy should be bought to be used, not to be admired from a distance. The very young child cannot possibly know that some toys will break if he mishandles them. In fact, he does not know he is mishandling them. Is it his fault if they break? If it is anyone's fault it is that of the grownup who gave him, say, a breakable doll instead of an unbreakable one.

It takes a long time for a child to acquire the skill and physical coordination to use a delicate or complicated object of any kind. At first he does not know his own strength, or how to control or direct it. That too he learns as he grows.

Is your child "old enough to know better"? How old that is depends not only on the individual child but also on his parental teaching. When parents do not themselves value and take care of things, the child is not likely to learn the value of his own things or take good care of them.

Are you trying to teach the child by scolding and threats? "Why didn't you take care of it? I told you so!" Some children can be intimidated by this sort of thing, crushed in spirit. Now and then a child will revolt against it by breaking other toys.

Here is another point to consider: Does your child like his toys? If he begs you to fix a toy that has broken, that toy means a lot to him. He is distressed and concerned about it. Because of this concern he becomes aware of the need for care when playing with it.

Suppose you do not wait for him to call your attention to the broken toy but immediately buy him another, and several more besides (it's hard to come away from a toy shop without a load). He may then not value his toys because, whether he cares or not for any one toy it is immediately replaced, plus bonus, when broken.

When the child is not concerned about the broken toy, it is proof that that toy didn't really interest him. He may not let you throw it away, however, for he has developed a sense of property. But unless he asks you to fix it, or to help him fix it, and is very distressed to learn that it can't be mended, do not buy him another of the same kind.

If your child is careless about his toys in that he scatters them about and does not put them away, you may be expecting too much of him too early. It is much harder for him to put things away than to take them out.

He will learn gradually and only when you help him put his things away.

Our three-year-old son plays with a baby doll. Does this mean he is going to be a sissy? Is it abnormal?

No. Boys under five as well as girls find pleasure and satisfaction in playing with dolls. Some parents tend to shame boys away from dolls. There is no reason for this except an unanalyzed feeling that little boys should be all male. Yet some little girls are tomboyish and we have ceased to be upset about that.

Let your little boy play with dolls. And don't be worried, either, if he is playing so-called "feminine" games with girl playmates he may have—House, Tea Party, and the like. They mean something to him. His interest will change naturally in kindergarten, if not before.

You can learn a lot by observing. If a little boy of three or older is getting great satisfaction out of a *baby* doll, it may be that he is not getting enough love and attention from Mother. With the doll baby he is projecting himself into the baby situation, while at the same time he is Mother or Daddy, giving himself (the doll) the love and attention he needs. You can frequently see what he is missing and yearning for by what he does with the doll. A little girl may do the same thing, but unfortunately it is often not noticed, just because she is a girl.

Do children need toys that make a lot of noise?

Many children like them. They need a few toys of this kind because they use them in different ways from other toys—rhythmically, for example. Rhythm is fascinating, whether children make it themselves or listen to it in music. A child's banging or tooting may not sound rhythmical or musical to you, but it generally does to him.

Just as a child has to run and jump and climb, so he has to shout and scream. The quiet child is the one to be most concerned about.

When your child's noise-making seems about to drive you out of your mind, think of the old slogan, "If you can't lick 'em, join 'em." Put on a record and dance with him. Or play a clapping verse game with him, such as "Pease porridge hot."

If your child is given a drum, horn, or whistle, be prepared for the worst. After all, what is a drum for but to be banged, a horn or whistle but to be blown?

To soften noise activities, you will have to gain your child's cooperation, asking him to save them for out-doors. Tell him the reasons. Given the reasons he will try to cooperate. However, he will forget, and will need an occasional reminder from you.

What kind of toys are best to take on long trips on a train or bus or in the car?

The kind of play materials you take on such a trip depends on the age of the child and the amount of space you have available for carrying them.

If he has his own small bag or basket that can be used for carrying them, he can of course put his things in that, and then he can open it whenever he wants to use something. Most children enjoy crayons, some drawing paper, blunt scissors, their favorite small car or doll, and one or two books. This variety will keep them occupied for quite a time.

In addition, it is a good idea to have a surprise for the child. This should be kept from him until you see that he is becoming restless and would welcome a new interest. Your surprise will give him something new to do and think about.

Select this surprise with care. It must be something that he can use in a variety of ways either in his lap or on the seat. It could be a package of pipe cleaners, a small doll wrapped in a blanket, an airplane, a tiny wheelbarrow, or some such thing which you are sure he will enjoy.

How much play space does a child need?

He can use as much play territory as you can spare him. Children must have room in which to use their muscles for growth in strength and coordination.

Have you ever observed how a child in a building with long corridors has an impulse to run? This is doubly true of children who live in cramped apartments. They feel so hemmed in that to them the long corridor immediately says *Run!* and off they go.

When school children pour out of their classrooms into the playground at recess, the noise they make is deafening, and their play at first is like a burst of fireworks—explosive. They are releasing pent-up energy. They are unlimbering.

A child has to be active. As he grows he tires less quickly and the range of his activities widens along with his ability to do more things. The little one who used to spend the greater part of his life sleeping outgrows his crib and needs a bed. His eating and sleeping schedule changes to approximate your own. He once crawled, then toddled; now he runs, jumps, and climbs.

Does he need to run, jump, and climb?

Indeed he does. Nature is driving him, demanding space for maneuver.

Add to that the fact that when boys and girls grow to grade school age they have an urge to shout and shriek. No game in which three or four are engaged can, apparently, be played quietly. They have to yell encouragement or disparagement or warning, and when there is no particular reason for communication, they yell for the fun of yelling. Reconcile yourself to the commotion; it's all a part of happy, growing children.

How can we let our child be active indoors when there just isn't an inch of extra space?

This is a common problem. Happy were the children able to grow up in the big roomy houses and grounds of Mark Twain's Tom Sawyer and Booth Tarkington's Penrod! We have progressed from that to "efficient" apartments and bungalows where practically every inch has been figured, as neat and unexpandable as a ship's cabin or a pullman roomette.

Well, you have to do what you can with what you have. To begin with: Have a good look. Is your house or apartment really small—or is it cluttered? Is it both small *and* cluttered?

Next: Is everything in it necessary, or are there some articles of furniture that can be stored?

Now: If it is small and everything in it really is needed, what can you accomplish by pushing one or two pieces of furniture to one side to make extra space available? When he finishes with his play you can make your child feel big and important if you let him help to move the furniture back into place.

Children aren't usually aware of their need for

space. They can't figure out why they aren't allowed to do certain things that require space indoors. They feel cramped without actually knowing what is bothering them. So they forget the stern "No!" or try to jump or climb when Mother isn't looking; or they become fretful. When you make it possible for them to have even a few extra square feet of play space, they feel happy about it.

In a manner of speaking, children do have to be kept tethered, but the longer the tether and the greater the browsing space, the better for them—and for you.

Is our child getting enough outdoor play?

No matter where you live you must get your child outdoors regularly, weather permitting. You begin this with the baby, taking him out in his carriage for a healthful change of air and scene. You continue with the toddler, and should, if you can, have a lightweight stroller for him because he'll be wanting to get in and out of it. He'll also like to push it.

Your older running–jumping–climbing child will be out by himself, playing with his friends.

If you have a community park or playground close by, you are fortunate. Too many children in town and city have to make do with the sidewalk in front of the house. The narrow sidewalk limits the big-muscle activities and there is always the danger that in the heat of play the child will forget himself and dart out into the street. Unless you can make your community take action in providing safe places for the children, there is no solution to this problem short of moving to a park neighborhood, the suburbs, or the country.

The younger child outdoors has special needs. The first of these is your company, because he can't get around well and has to be watched. He needs to push, and enjoys pushing his stroller or baby carriage. He needs to pull, and there are pull-toys for him on a long handle or rope. Some of the best are the kind that come with a built-in noise so that the child knows it is there behind him and doesn't have to be twisting around all the time to make sure.

Incidentally, indoors or out, children under five have hardly any sense of time. The under-five child needs to take his time, and the younger he is the more time margin he needs. He is bound to toddle along at his own pace and needs to be able to stop and examine interesting things in his new wide world. It doesn't help very much for you to try to hurry him. This is particularly so when he is getting dressed, putting up his toys, or getting ready for bed. The concept of hours, minutes, and seconds is just not a part of his understanding.

Often when you scoop him up to hug or cuddle or carry him he will squirm and try to wriggle away. Many exciting things demand his attention, including the wonderful experiences of standing and moving about on his own two feet. At such times let him alone; give him time to accomplish whatever he is doing.

Our little girl doesn't like to play outdoors. When we send her out she stands near the door and cries. How can we help her?

Don't just send her out—go with her. Something may be troubling her. It may be that she is afraid she will find you gone when she returns; there may have been such an experience in her past. It may be that you have given her the feeling that punishment is involved. "Go out and play!" is too often the command of an impatient mother.

Does your little girl have outdoor play materials such as a tricycle, wagon, doll carriage, sandbox, swing, and the like? Is her problem one of not being able to think of anything to do when she gets outdoors? Does she have friends to play with when she is there? Does she cry because she wants you to come out and play with her? As you answer these four questions, you may find the answer to why she does not want to play outdoors. If you suggest an activity for her to do outside, she may run off and do it and then come inside as soon as she has finished. Once she has had some fun doing one thing, even though it takes her only a few minutes, she will be less hesitant about going out the next time. There will be times when you will want to go out with her and help her learn to enjoy one or two new activities. Of course, if you have a baby in the house, it is not always possible for you to go out. If this is the case, try to plan the outdoor play period for your older child at a time you can take the baby with you.

When our child has to stay indoors we just let him watch television as long as he wants. Is this wrong?

Many parents do this because it is for them a solution. You don't have to keep an eye on the child who is glued to the television set. He seems safe, and he's not getting into mischief. Also, you don't have to think of things for him to do.

This is unfortunate. The child who is encouraged and helped to develop resourcefulness is building up creative ability and has many important little triumphs of achievement. He learns to value objects, and he also learns to value himself, because he can make and make-do. These experiences will serve him in many ways as he grows older.

Television should have a place in his life—in fact, you can't and don't want to keep him from it. This home screen is a great source of pleasure and fascination, and can enrich the child's life. But if he watches TV programs a good part of the day, he is not using his body but only his eyes, and he is not very actively using his mind. What is more, he may begin to demand the use of the set as his right, without considering others. Mother wants to watch her favorite programs and Daddy his and brothers and sisters theirs—so there will be squabbles.

You can't forbid your child television. Nowadays the three things children spend the greatest amount of time doing are sleeping, attending school, and watching television.

How can we use television wisely with our child?

It may seem an impossible task, but truly it is not. It does mean that you will have to do some guiding and planning with your child.

Set aside a time during the week end to work out with your child a schedule of programs for his viewing, and ask for his cooperation so that he abides by the schedule both for his own sake and in consideration for the other members of the family.

This of course can seldom be done with children under six. For them, each day's viewing may be planned at breakfast or shortly after.

The older child will enjoy going over the magazine or newspaper lists of the week's programs and studying them with you. There will be much discussion. You will be encouraging your child's opinion even when you disagree with it. If you disagree strongly, you must explain why you would rather not have him look at this or that program which he wants to see. If he insists, and the program comes within his viewing time schedule, watch that program with him.

The child who is old enough to read and study with you the week's programs, is also old enough to have his opinions, tastes, and feelings respected. They are not experienced tastes and opinions, as yours are. But when there is good—which means, not disapproving or scornful—family discussion, your child can learn to respect the opinions of others while keeping his own.

Your child will have his favorite programs, just as you have yours. If his favorites are all of one kind, suggest that he watch a different kind just for a change, and also because he may find he likes it and has been missing something. Variety will enrich his life and broaden his interests. Program-viewing should be, as far as possible, a balanced experience.

Young children (like many grownups) want at least one program with a day-to-day sequence—a program with which they identify themselves, and which gives them a sense of being participants in what is taking place. The best kind is one that gives them many ideas for activities which they may carry on after the program is finished.

If your child is torn between two programs of equal interest that go on at the same time, he knows very well that he can't see them both. Help him make up his own mind, but do not make the decision for him.

If he wants to watch a program that interferes with meals, homework, or bedtime, you and he can plan for this occasionally, but it must not become a regular activity.

Give him every opportunity and encouragement to talk about the programs he sees. He is having real experiences in viewing, and it is best for both of you if you share them. He also learns in this way to talk well—to narrate and describe. Besides, he may have misunderstandings which you can clarify.

Television should never take the place of outdoor play, indoor play and work, reading books, or listening to records. In general, the child's own self-directed activity is always preferable to passive on-looking. It is on the whole just as important for him to play a mouth organ or ring a triangle as it is to listen to music.

Nor should you let your child use it merely to keep him quiet or out of the way. In this sense TV can be a "silencer," and it should be used sparingly for that purpose. Instead use this ingenious invention for its great good—to share with your child the manifold things it offers, to encourage and stimulate his thinking, to enrich his life and your own.

✻⤳❂⤷✻⤳❂⤷✻⤳❂⤷✻⤳❂⤷✻⤳❂

The magic of books and storytelling

✻⤳❂⤷✻⤳❂⤷✻⤳❂⤷✻⤳❂⤷✻⤳❂

When should we introduce our child to books?

You can begin when your child is eight to ten months old.

Does this seem very young? It isn't when you understand what to expect.

Your child will not take the book, hold it right-side-up, turn the pages, and so on. Do not expect him to use it as you do—not for a long time. You have been introducing him to many objects. The book is, to him, just another object. He will feel it, pull and tug at it. He may even try to put the corners in his mouth.

There are many large picture books printed especially for very young children. The pages are of linen or a plastic-coated material that won't tear. For the child's first books it is essential that you get this indestructible kind.

Remember that your youngster is tearing up magazines when he gets hold of them. He's going to try to tear up books also during this pull–tug–tear period.

You don't want him to feel that the books are "Mustn't touch!" things. You want him to love them. Books are going to be important to him all his life, taking him into a wonderland of pleasure, new experiences, and of learning.

So from the very beginning give your child the feeling that books are both special and wonderful. You can help do this just by feeling it yourself. And if in this early period you keep your own books out of his reach, like other valuable things, you won't be having to warn, "Mustn't touch!"

How should we introduce him to books?

The time you save or set aside for this purpose should be a time when you are relaxed, when you can share fully in this great new experience he is about to enter.

I stress the point that you should be relaxed because, from the beginning, showing your child how to use books involves teaching and training as well as fun for both of you. Unhurried time and loving patience are necessary.

Show him the book, turning the pages and staying at each page just as long as he is interested—which at first may be only a few seconds or a minute. Point out things in the pictures—boy, girl, baby, shoe, hat, and so on.

Let him feel and handle the book; that is the only way he can get to know it at this time. But when he tries to use it like any other toy, explain to him that a book is to be looked at and enjoyed, not pulled apart. If he is not interested, put the book away and try again another day.

It may take weeks or months of consistent explaining on your part before the child realizes that these new things called books are not to be banged about.

It may also take time for his eyes to focus on pictures and for his mind to become aware of what they are. He likes the pictures and colors and wants physical contact with them. He may look at you to see if it's all right to pat the lovely pictures.

These first books should be easy to handle, because learning to turn the pages is a challenge to a young child. He feels he can do it, and he wants to. When you are turning a page, pause to see if he wants to complete the turning.

At about eighteen months, if you hold the book steady for him, he can turn pages all by himself. He's not yet skillful at it and will turn several at a time. In another few months he will be able to turn one page at a time.

Meanwhile he stops to look at pictures you point out to him, or he points out a picture to you. You ask questions: "Where is the baby? See the dog. What is the dog doing?" And you read part of the story to him.

When your child can see a book and let it lie without trying to pull it apart, he can also pick it up and put it down. He will be bringing it to you for you to show him his favorite pictures.

When you and your child are enjoying books together is the time to show him how to pick up a book from the table or shelf. Tell him to be sure the book is closed before he picks it up. In this way he learns not to lift or carry the book by its pages or cover, which may tear.

You have now taught your child what a book is, what it is for, how to handle it, and how to take care of it. You have trained him to good habits and a sense of value about books. And by means of the contents of the books, you have helped him to increase his vocabulary and stimulated his responses—in short, you have widened his world. You have been laying the foundations of a lifelong friendship between him and books.

And with all this, you and your child have been having a fine time.

What books should we buy?

For the first three years, children need books that have short stories built around everyday experiences. They identify themselves and form close friendships with the characters in the books. They can see themselves doing the things the children in the stories are doing. It is to them something like looking into a mirror, but more fascinating.

After a child reaches the age of three, his books become more important in helping enlarge and enrich his interests. At this age children are most interested in learning about the "real" world. They like stories about steam shovels, children of other lands, and animals they do not often see such as lions, zebras, monkeys, and elephants. They also like stories about boats, airplanes, clouds, houses.

In buying books you may feel dependent on the book clerk's advice, or the publisher's advertising, or a book review you have read stating for what age group the particular book was written. You may also get excellent advice and book lists from the librarian of the children's room in your public library.

You must still use your own best judgment, however. Base this judgment on three rules:

1. The story should not be frightening. You know your own child. Never mind what is recommended for

children in general. If there is anything in the story which you feel may frighten him, pass it by. There are plenty of books.

2. The illustrations should be interesting and colorful, but not grotesque.

3. The contents should not be misleading. If it is a "real" story, things should be as they are in life. "Pretend" elements should not enter. When you have fanciful stories, tell your child, "This is a 'pretend' story," but see first that nothing in it is frightening.

It is a good idea to pass on the three rules of book-gift giving to relatives.

On birthdays or at other times, young children sometimes receive books that are too advanced for them, or which might contain frightening and confusing stories such as we find in many fairy tales. If you realize that a book is too advanced for your child, don't make a negative comment to him about it and then take it away. Read one or two pages to him in a monotonous voice so that the story sounds boring, and you will see how quickly he loses interest in the book. "You don't want to hear any more of this story now, do you? Then, let's put it away," you might say. He will be in complete agreement with you. Several months or even a year later, when you think that he can understand and enjoy the book give it to him again.

Incidentally, when you like reading to your child, bring the book and read with enthusiasm. When you like the story, you can be pretty sure that he will like it too.

When is a child old enough to be taken to the public library?

It is not necessary to wait until your child is in the first grade and beginning to read. Many children at the age of four are ready for the library and should be taken there quite regularly. The public library can be a fascinating place for your child. And your first visit to the library together will be heartwarming for you as well.

Many libraries have children's rooms or sections, furnished with low tables and chairs. The books are specially arranged for children and the librarian is helpful. Both you and the librarian will quickly see if your child fully understands how to handle books. As early as the age of four, many children are selecting the books that appeal to them. On his first visit to the library the child should not be expected to sit quietly and look at or read a book, however. This comes later.

In many public libraries the children's librarian conducts a story hour at least once a week. Your child can have a wonderful time and an excellent new sort of experience at these story sessions.

Can a child have too many books?

While it is possible for a child to have too many toys and consequently not appreciate any of them fully, the same does not hold true for a child's feeling for books.

Children of all ages have their favorite books, but this does not mean that they are not interested in others. They look at their favorite books over and over. Young children ask you to read the same story to them day after day.

Then there are the books children enjoy for a while and put away for a few months or a year. The books which they enjoyed looking at and hearing you read to them when they were very young, they enjoy again when they are learning to read. A new feeling of personal accomplishment, combined with affection for the book, comes when they can read these stories by themselves or with your help.

Don't buy books for your child simply to surround him with them. Each new book should be selected with care and with the child's interests and wishes in mind.

Should we teach our child to read?

No. Years ago all children were taught to read and write by the same method. It began with learning the alphabet. In those days parents helped their preschool children by teaching them the alphabet.

Today, however, this cannot be done. Different methods have been developed. It has been found that some children have had difficulty learning to read because their parents had started them off with the method used when they themselves were in first grade, and the school their children are attending uses a different method. These children became confused and found learning to read a very difficult task.

So it is very important that you let the trained teacher initiate your child into reading. When you understand the technique used in your child's school, you can help at home.

If you don't understand the technique, don't be annoyed with your child's teacher. The method by which each of us learned to read formed a mental pattern so deep that it may be difficult to understand a different one. If you can't understand, just let your child lead the way. Then at a later time consult the teacher about her methods and your child's progress.

Our child has little interest in books or reading. Is this abnormal?

It is unfortunate.

Much has been written about "reading readiness"— a term applied to the child's developing a desire to read long before he enters school.

This development does not occur in just the few weeks or even the few months before his first-grade experience begins. It includes all the years in which the child has been hearing you tell and read him stories, beginning with infancy. It is during these early years that his interest in the printed word is formed. A child between the ages of five and six sees the bold headlines on a newspaper and tries to read them. When he can't figure out what they say he will tug at his mother's skirt or his daddy's trousers and say, "Read it to me." When he rides in the car he will ask similar questions about billboards.

Children cannot learn to read unless they really want to. They need to have this desire and interest in order to be able to coordinate all their efforts upon a learning process which is more highly concentrated and challenging than anything they have experienced thus far.

You are the key person in helping your child to create this great desire to want to read. His teachers in school are the ones to actually teach him how to read.

Your enthusiasm for reading *to* your child is very important. But there is another equally important factor. Your child needs to see you yourself reading and enjoying your own books and magazines. He needs to see and feel through you the joys, excitement, and interest of reading. This is what raises his level of "reading readiness" to the point that he is happy and impatient to learn to read.

In bringing up your child, do not send him off to sit in a chair or to his room to look at books or read because of some mischief he has done. Do not link books to punishment in his mind. If you do you can easily give him a negative feeling toward books. And that, of course, is the opposite goal from the one you really want.

Our child often asks us to tell him a story rather than read one. Can you give us some storytelling techniques?

Mr. Ames is one of the many young parents who has discussed storytelling with me. He didn't understand why a child wants "home-made" stories when those in books are so delightful and entertaining.

Mr. Ames felt that he was failing his daughter by not telling her any stories. "But I just go blank!" he added. "I honestly don't know any stories to tell her."

Parents who feel they are unable to tell stories to their children are usually thinking of a story as something with scenes, a cast of characters, and a plot. They think in terms of book, magazine, movie, and television stories. But this is not what the young child wants when he says, "Tell me a story."

What does he want?

He wants you to tell him a short story that he will understand and enjoy because there are only one or two people in the story and they do things that are familiar to him.

For example, the story could go like this: "I know a little girl whose name is Jennifer [use your child's name]. She has brown hair and big brown eyes. Her favorite dessert is baked apple. Sometimes she likes to pour milk over it.

"Jennifer is a very happy little girl. She likes to play

with her daddy. She likes to help her mother get dinner. One day Jennifer went for a walk with her daddy. They saw a squirrel run up a tree. I like Jennifer."

A short story like that will please Jennifer because she knows it is about her. When she realizes that the story has ended she may ask you to repeat it or she may say, "Tell me more." If she desires more, all you have to do is add another experience or two that you know Jennifer has enjoyed.

Young children want you to tell them stories about the things children do. Sometimes you may add a fanciful aspect to it and your child will laugh because he understands the pretense in it. Other times your child may take the story and add more to it purely for your entertainment.

Once you have gotten over the fear and hesitation of making up stories you will enjoy doing it, and you and your child will have much fun together. You will want to do it often and instead of waiting for him to invite you to tell a story you will hear yourself saying: "Come over and sit on my knee and I will tell you a story."

One day you may be hard put to it when your child says, "Tell me the story about the little girl who danced with you." You can't remember the one she is thinking of so you start making up a new one. She interrupts you by saying, "No, that is not the right one." Children remember the stories you tell them and they have their favorites which they will ask you to repeat. So try to remember them, if you can.

Infants love to hear their parents tell them stories and recite rhymes. A good time for this is while you are bathing, dressing, feeding, playing with, and getting a baby ready for bed. You will enjoy them along with the child. Tell the best of the Mother Goose rhymes, some jingles, and make up simple stories of your own. You will be surprised at what an excellent storyteller you become.

Do older children still like to have stories told to them?

Indeed they do. The subject matter should be in keeping with their new interests and should include a number of details and perhaps more humorous aspects.

Five-, six-, and seven-year-olds like to have you make up a story about a picture they have made. Or they may want to draw pictures to illustrate a story that you have told them.

These children also like to start a story and then have you finish it. Or the reverse: you start the story and let them finish it. It may become a routine of taking turns.

About this time children may ask you to write the story on paper as they tell it to you. Then they will draw the pictures to go with the story. You will be asked to staple it together so that it looks like a book. Some children have a large collection of such books of original stories.

I know a number of children who save this making of original stories into books for the week end when it becomes a regular father–child activity. Both father and child look forward to this.

There are two cautions and one rule to keep in mind when you are telling stories:

Caution 1: Tell no story that might breed fear.

Caution 2: The lecture or lesson story, or the scolding type of story, will not accomplish what you want to teach and will contribute greatly to making your child less interested in stories. This may stifle his interest in books and learning to read.

Rule: A story is to be enjoyed by both listener and teller.

We think our child spends too much time with books. How can we interest him in other things?

It is very important that a child have a wide variety of interests and activities. Books should not be his only interest. First, let's think about why he prefers books to other activities:

1. What kind of play space does he have, both in the house and outdoors? If he is so limited that he feels he cannot do the things he wants to do, he may have become discouraged and turned to books.

2. Does he have friends of his age and size with

whom he can play frequently? Or is he isolated from other children most of the time, seeing them only occasionally?

3. Have you found it easier to provide a shelf for his books than to provide storage space for his toys and therefore unconsciously given him more books than toys?

There could be many reasons why your child prefers books. However, rather than wait until you find one or a combination of reasons, start now to interest him in other activities. This may mean taking him on a series of short excursions—to a museum, to see a large ship at the pier, to the airport to see how many different kinds of planes there are, to the greenhouse to discover how things grow, and many other interesting places. Follow these trips with the two of you building an airport from blocks, boxes and boards, or creating a picture of what you saw, each of you taking turns at putting something else into the picture.

In opening new interests and activities for your child, however, be very careful not to destroy his interest in books and reading. Never let him know that you think he spends too much time reading and looking at books. First bring the new projects to him through suggesting and then planning these excursions with him. Encourage him to think of more places to go and new things to discover.

He will soon find that he doesn't have quite as much time to spend with books because there are so many other interesting things to do. As a result he will feel better physically and mentally because he is up and about more. Also, he will enjoy the books he reads with even more enthusiasm than he had in the past.

When should we let our child browse through our good books?

When the very young child is first learning what books are and what to do with them, keep him away from your bookshelves. This is the time when the toddler is finding out about everything but doesn't have the bodily coordination or the understanding to handle books with care.

By the time your child is two and a half or three years old he has learned how to handle books carefully. He appreciates what is between the covers of a book. When you see this to be true it is time to take down the barriers of "Don't touch!" Without making a lesson of it or issuing a special invitation to go to your bookshelf, tell him that you have many wonderful books that belong to Mother and Daddy. Some have pictures, others do not. He might like to have you show him one of your books.

The first few times he looks at your books it should be under your supervision. He will not find them very interesting; therefore these experiences will not come too frequently.

As he grows older he may want to browse through your books more often. He should ask your permission to do so; this is a basic principle when he wants to use something that belongs to another member of the family. You should comply with his request so long as he shows that he can handle the books carefully.

Such browsing through books, even though they are not written for his age or interest, stimulates a new appreciation for books and their place in family living and the whole world of reading and learning.

Is it better to buy individual books or a set of books?

Children need both.

The child's first experiences are with individual books which have one or two stories. As his experience widens, he has an interest in books which have several different stories about the same subject or different subjects.

By the time your child is seven or eight years old he is ready for a first set of books to which he can go for information. This first encyclopedia set should be selected with care in terms of accuracy, durability, and usability. It must be so organized that the child will find it not only easy but also satisfying to use.

When your child has an encyclopedia and several anthologies which contain many of his favorite stories, it is just as important for him to have a variety of new individual books. One kind of book never replaces another in the life of a child who is reading and seeking new ideas and more information.

Should we read all the books that our child reads?

Many parents ask this question. By choice you would like to be familiar with all the material your child reads. You may even feel that you would like to read the books before your child gets to them, censor some of the material, and suggest different books.

It is not necessary for you to read everything that your child reads. By the time he is reading newspapers, magazines, and books he is not doing all of it at home. He reads at school, Sunday school, with friends, and in many other places. It is impossible for you to read everything that he reads.

However, it is essential for you to have an active interest in the different kinds of material that your child reads. Discuss them with him, thus giving him the opportunity to tell you about the ones he finds most interesting and those least meaningful.

Even though he may read some books or magazines of which you disapprove, let him discuss them with you freely. This way you can guide his thinking concerning what he has read. If you openly disapprove of this material he may feel that he can't tell you about it and read it away from home.

There will be times when your child will ask you to read a book or story that he has finished. When this happens it is important that you do so; he is telling you that he would like to talk about it. He wants your reactions and ideas.

Does requiring our eight-year-old to read a specific number of pages each day help him or confuse him?

Why have you given him this assignment in the first place? Is it because he is not reading as well as you or his teacher think he should? Is it a disciplinary measure because you think that he spends too much time at play and too little reading? Do you give him a number of pages on a certain subject or just any pages, as long as he reads the number you have indicated?

Such requirements given to an eight- or twelve-year-old must be thought through very carefully. Will they accomplish what you want for your child?

My experience has been that a required number of pages, whether two or twenty, does not produce the desired goal. Asking a child to read a short story or an article in a magazine or newspaper often produces much better results.

The specific number of pages may leave the child with an unfinished story. This doesn't give him the feeling of having accomplished something. Reading an entire short story does give him the feeling that he started and completed the story in one sitting.

If you are planning to give your child such home assignments, be sure that you discuss this with his teacher first. Without such clearance you may start something which at home seems fine but which creates a problem for your child in school.

*❧❀❧✿❧✿❧✿❧✿❧✿❧✿❧✿❧❀

FIVE

We guide our child

*❧❀❧✿❧✿❧✿❧✿❧✿❧✿❧❀

Why do young children say "No!" and "I won't!"?

They are trying these words out, and they are trying you out too, not always realizing what they are doing.

The commanding negative a child hears so often from adults is one of the first ideas he begins to grasp. It is very persuasive. It stops him in mid-motion, or it stops him at the very beginning of an action when both mind and body are impelling him to that action.

It is when their child first says "No" to them that many parents have difficulties with themselves. They tend to be shocked or angry. The child seems to them disrespectful or impudent. Some parents respond with "Don't you dare talk back to me!"

It helps when such occasions arise if parents know that the child is trying out what he has learned from them. The child is not simply being disrespectful or impudent. In fact, in trying out his "Won't!" he is taking one of his first steps in the direction of independence —in asserting himself and communicating feelings and wishes in speech.

Should we accept our child's "No!" and "I won't!"?

Stop and think about what is happening.

A clash of wills may be involved. The child's will is "willful." He does not have the experience and thoughtfulness which should be behind the adult "No." You, however, do have the background of experience and wisdom. So when necessary you override his refusal or rejection—not in a temper, but kindly and firmly.

Take Mr. and Mrs. Blake. Their four-year-old son was playing with total absorption when bedtime was at hand. Mrs. Blake said, "Bobby, it is time for you to go to bed. Stop playing now and go upstairs." Bobby ignored her. Mr. Blake immediately rose from his chair and advanced upon his son. Bobby began to scream, "No! No!" Struggling furiously in his father's arms, he was carried off and from the bedroom I heard the noisy and prolonged protest.

If Mrs. Blake had said, "Bobby, you will have five

minutes to finish what you are doing and then it will be your bedtime. I will tell you when the five minutes are finished," Bobby would have had fair warning and would probably have complied amiably.

Naptime and bedtime should be a normal part of the child's daily routine. Then, on the occasions when he does not want to go to bed when you ask him, there is usually a reason. Perhaps you have guests with whom he wants to continue to visit, or maybe he thinks something is about to happen which he doesn't want to miss. Assure him that in the morning you will tell him all about what happened after he went to bed. This will usually take care of the situation, and, of course, you should keep your promise.

A child soon learns that when he says "No" to his father or mother it doesn't work the way it does when Mother or Father says "No" to him.

From his point of view, this seems unfair. Yet it is something he must learn to accept. When authority is imposed in a firm but friendly manner, he can accept it more easily. He grows into the understanding that "No!" as a command is based on careful consideration, judgment, and mature wisdom.

Of course, when you yourself say "No," you must mean it.

My friends the Pruits enjoy recalling the day that Barbara, who is now grown up, made one of her greatest discoveries. It was a hot summer morning. She had been asking and then begging to be allowed outdoors without any clothes on. Her mother kept saying "No." Barbara tried it once more, and this time got a very emphatic "*No!*" There was a moment of complete silence. Then Barbara looked up at her mother and said clearly and solemnly, "When you say 'no,' you don't mean 'yes'!"

Barbara fully understood.

An angry parental response to a child's "No" often arouses in him the same feelings, for anger is contagious. When angry punishment follows he is also frightened.

When this happens he learns that it is not wise to say "No" to his parents. He tries it out on others, and because he usually does so with the same anger his parents have shown toward him, he learns that it is also not smart to say "No" to anyone bigger or stronger than himself.

The ability to say "No" and "I won't" at the proper time throughout life is a very important one. The child who can say this to friends who want him to join in activities he knows are wrong shows great strength of character.

Children should be encouraged by their parents to use "No" in the right way. You do this first of all by keeping your own "No" clear and firm, saying it only when necessary. But you can also invite your child's opinion, as often as possible. In this way you encourage thought, discrimination, and judgment—all of which are necessary for the right use of "No," and also the right kind of "Yes."

Guidance is the mainspring of discipline. It is wise and loving leadership not only for the present but also looking ahead to the future.

How can we teach our child to put away his toys?

Do not demand and expect too much too soon. The young child can take things out much more easily than he can put them away. Putting away is actually hard to learn.

We know that for a young child, something that is out of sight is gone. If it is something he is fond of, and you put it away in a chest or closet, he may protest bitterly.

He loves to have his favorite toy or doll within easy reach because it is so reassuring to know it is there, not gone. If, instead, you put it away, he is going to be deeply troubled. He can't be certain it will be there tomorrow, as you say it will. "Tomorrow" for the child is a never-never time. He has no real conception of it.

There should be wall space available in your child's room. Open shelves are the best place to keep his toys. If possible, the shelves should be deep enough to hold the larger toys as well as the smaller.

When the child can see his toys, he does not object to your putting them away. It then becomes easier for you to teach him to put them away himself, because no troubled feeling stands in the way.

The shelves should be low, so that the child can get at all his toys. Many a mother discovers that the toy away up there is the one Johnny just has to have, this very minute. Often when she brings it down for him, he abandons it almost immediately.

If your child does this, he is letting you know as best he can that he needs to feel these precious possessions are *his*—not yours, or the shelf's. It is good for him to have this feeling. It helps him to assume responsibility for his possessions.

When your child has a great many toys, it is harder for him to learn to put them away. More work is involved. He tires quickly or is distracted by something more interesting to do. A heap of toys spread all over the floor seems overwhelming to the young child when it comes to picking them up.

The child who is fond of his toys is upset when a toy is lost or broken. You are familiar—or very soon will be—with a child's look of reproach or cry of angry accusation when an adult accidentally steps or sits on the toy or game which he has carelessly left about. While sympathizing with his distress, you explain that this is bound to happen when the toys are not kept in their proper place. It is in a situation such as this that the lesson of cause and effect begins to take hold. It is a lesson of experience.

When the adults in the household have orderly habits, the child learns further through imitation. To demand of him more than you do of yourself or of others in the family is obviously unjust. Also, standards that are too high for him to carry through are so frustrating that he is apt to run away from the situation.

How can we teach our child to put away his clothes?

First: The hooks, hangers, and drawers must be within his reach. Lower the clothes rack in his closet so that he can reach it easily. If he shares a bureau with you or with older brothers or sisters, set aside the lower drawers for his clothes.

Second: Encourage your child to feel that his clothes are his very own possessions, just as his toys are. He should have clothes that he likes and enjoys. When it is time to dress, ask him what he would like to wear. If what he chooses is not suitable, you will have to explain why. As early as possible, take your child along with you when you are shopping for him. However, if you must shop at the same time for other things that have nothing to do with him (as is often the case), it is better not to do this. Boredom makes him restless and his whining will make you tense.

Third: Make sure that the other members of the family are putting away their clothes. You cannot expect your child to feel that tidy habits are important if he sees that someone else in the family doesn't think so.

Fourth: When your child is old enough to put away his clothes and is learning the habit, he will now and then forget. If he leaves his clothes on a chair or on the floor, remind him by saying, "Oh, what did you forget to do?" or "Somebody forgot to do something." Scolding, punishment, or nagging will make tidying up a disagreeable chore and will delay this learning process.

Our ten-year-old daughter never picks up her things or hangs up her clothes. What do you advise?

You can begin to tackle the problem by asking yourself:

1. Are my standards for her so high that she has given up completely?

2. Have I been nagging her? (Nagging has a curious effect. The nagged person "turns a deaf ear"; she actually does develop a self-protective deafness.)

3. Is my daughter leaving her things on the chairs and floor in order to get more attention from me, even though it is in scolding?

4. How long has she been doing this? When did it begin? (If you can think back, you may be able to trace the source of the trouble.)

5. What have I been doing to help her overcome this difficulty?

You can do something to help both yourself and your daughter. Simply forget about her untidiness for the present. Then, when you start again, do it with a different approach. Help her in a friendly rather than in a scolding manner. Let her get the good feeling of having a neat room and the satisfaction that comes when she can find what she wants because she knows where she put it. Compliment her as often as you can.

And if her untidiness does not completely disappear? Is it really so grave that it cannot be overlooked? Many adults are untidy in varying degrees, too. Are they unpleasant or "bad" people?

One of my acquaintances is a very successful writer whose study would make a tidy housekeeper ill. His wife is careful to keep away from that room. The children have been taught that this is Daddy's special place. They may knock on the door and call to him whenever they need or want him, but they may not enter unless he invites them in. This man cannot work in a tidy room. Nobody thinks less of him because of it. His working habits are not tidy—his mind is.

How can we keep our son from jumping on the furniture?

By giving the child a clear, firm explanation that this is something he cannot do, that furniture belongs to all the family and is not made for that kind of play.

When children are forced to stay indoors they become restless and look around for things to do. They gravitate naturally toward climbing and jumping, because such activity exercises the large muscles and helps release their great store of energy. (You know yourself that when you are feeling full of life and are "tied down," you become irritable.)

It is always a good idea to have a number of things for the children to do when they must stay indoors. Participate as much as possible, at least to the point of giving them a good start. You can dance with your child to the music of records or radio. You can teach him bending and stretching exercises.

What is your child's age? The three-, four-, and five-year-olds love to help with the housework and do well the assignments you give them. They like to push the vacuum cleaner (if it isn't too big or heavy for them) and the carpet sweeper. They enjoy helping make the beds, set the table and clear away, wash fresh fruit and vegetables, mop the floor, hold the dustpan while you sweep, wipe pots and pans—dishes too, of course, but not good china or crystal.

Young children like "real" jobs but they need your supervision. You will find these children of genuine help in some household chores.

Many older children enjoy helping, too, even though they seem to have discovered the difference between chores and fun. Louise, at six, keeps begging her mother to let her wash her own socks and underwear. And why isn't she permitted to do it? Because her mother thinks she is too young. I think that in this situation the mother is missing an important point. This is precisely a time when a willing child should be encouraged. Six-year-old Louises can be easily supervised. Not too strictly

—trustingly. If she messes up the bathroom, help her in a positive way, for her attitude is good and constructive. You want to help her do the job well, so she may learn eventually the task of taking responsibility for her own clothes.

Why do some children lie?

Children under six are in the stages of learning and absorbing the differences between reality and make-believe, truth and fiction, "mine" and "yours." They make mistakes and have misunderstandings which sometimes become lies. But after this period we can expect them to tell the truth.

In court, the defendant is always presumed innocent until proved guilty. All of us who live or work with children should abide by this principle. No one is born honest or dishonest. We have all had to learn the basic moral understandings and obligations—the agreements of fairness and justice by which the world lives.

A child who tells a lie once is not a liar. If you treat him thereafter with suspicion, he will lose confidence in himself. When you trust him, he is strengthened.

How can we help our child be truthful?

Honesty is a basic principle. Whether or not your child tells you the truth depends in great part on your reaction to his early mistakes and misunderstandings in the realm of honesty. When a child has made a mistake, he must, with your guidance, suffer the consequences. But the consequences must not be too much for him to bear, nor so light that he will think nothing of doing the same thing again.

Consider the story of Mrs. Manley and her son David.

Four-year-old David proudly brought his mother a bunch of freshly picked tulips. She accepted them, saying, "These are beautiful tulips! They look just like the ones Mrs. Reed is growing in her yard."

She had known immediately from their short stems that David must have picked them himself, probably without permission. Something of her dismay crept into her tone, for David looked at her doubtfully, a little fearfully.

At that moment, if Mrs. Manley had indicated that she accused and condemned him, David might—probably would—have lied. But his mother was friendly, and so, while he did sense that he had done something wrong, he replied truthfully to her question, "Did you get them from over there?" Yes, he had.

David's mother explained to him that he had made a mistake, because the flowers did not belong to him. She said, "We must do what we can about it. We will take the tulips back to Mrs. Reed, and you will tell her you are sorry and won't do it again."

It was a difficult situation because Mrs. Reed was

rather formidable about her tulips, and it was not going to be easy for Mrs. Manley to face her neighbor with the damage done to the tulip beds. But David must not know this. He had to learn to accept the consequences of mistakes. He could not be asked to do it alone while Mother waited for him at home. He had to carry the responsibility, but with his mother beside him, to help him if necessary.

Mother and son went together to their neighbor. When Mrs. Reed came to the door, he handed the bouquet to her. At her angry look he retreated a step. But his mother was there behind him, and she said, firmly and pleasantly, "David has something to tell you." The child's apology was not very coherent, and Mrs. Reed was not very cordial or sympathetic.

When they returned home they sat down and talked the situation over. His mother then asked David to play quietly in his room for a while, but not as punishment. He needed this time, after such a bewildering and upsetting experience—time to think. His mother felt confident that in the future he would remember, whenever he was playing outside, not to take anything that belonged to someone else.

If Mrs. Manley had herself taken the tulips back to Mrs. Reed, or if she had refused to accept her own responsibilities because she did not want to face Mrs. Reed, David would not have had so much to think about. Nor would he have begun to understand the meaning of what he had done.

Before you go too far in deciding whether you can trust your child, let's reverse the question. Ask yourself this:

Can you recall ever telling your child a lie? Did you ever ask him to lie for *you?*

On first thought, these are impertinent questions. But on second thought, can you recall ever telling your child that something was "all gone" because you didn't want him to have any more? Do you remember whether you told him that the Easter bunny laid hen's eggs? Did you ever ask him to tell the salesman at the door that you were not home? Did your child ever hear you tell someone an untruth that he must have known was such— refusing an invitation by saying you were having guests that night, for instance, when he knew no one had been invited?

I do not mean to say that children necessarily learn to lie from their parents. They may learn from many sources. In any case, they need a lot of your help in learning to stay with the truth.

I knew a six-year-old who told several lies in attempts to get the things he wanted. He couldn't understand why, in each instance, the truth became known, and he was then in trouble. Therefore I told him: "A lie has short legs. It can't run fast, so it always gets caught."

He understood this. It helped him crystallize his thinking, and with further consistent guidance this boy learned fully that truth was best.

Isn't discipline the same as punishment?

No. Do not confuse discipline with punishment. Mrs. Ward's problem with her daughter Margaret illustrates the difference between the two.

Mrs. Ward asked, as have many others, "Why does my child do something that she knows is wrong and then not help solve the problem?" What she really wanted to know was this: "When Margaret spills her milk on the floor or has any similar accident, she runs into the other room instead of cleaning up the mess. What can I do with her?"

"Why does Margaret run?" I asked.

When we talked it over we soon found the answer: Margaret ran because she was afraid. She knew she had done something wrong. She ran into the other room to get away from "the scene of the accident."

Many an adult "runs" when he does the same thing —knocking off an object from the store shelf, for example. Many another, for the same reason, tells a lie. I know a young man who does this. He is being groomed by his father to take over the business, a small but flourishing company. The father is deeply disturbed not only because his son occasionally makes a costly mistake, but mainly because then he denies that he did it. He lies, even though it is perfectly clear that he cannot possibly escape detection.

Why doesn't he confess and face the music? Because he is doing just what six-year-old Margaret is doing. He is running into the other room with the hope that someone else will clear up the situation. Now that he is grown, the "other room" is not out there but in his mind.

When punishment is confused with discipline, and substituted for discipline, the child does not learn to be "good." What he learns is that when he does wrong he will be punished.

Children will not all act the same in this life-situation. There are those who run. Some run very far; they run away from home. Others rebel, and the rebellion can take any form, one of which is joining a neighborhood gang that does lawless acts in defiance of both parents and the world. Some children become subdued and very, very good, in the wrong way—too good for their own good! They are usually socially handicapped because others dislike them and they are not truly happy with themselves. Other children become dependent, some almost to the point of helplessness. They are afraid to do anything at all because they may do it wrong and be punished.

Margaret's mother knew that Margaret was not "bad." Yet in guiding her she had acted just as if her daughter's mistakes and accidents were in fact "badness." The fact that Margaret ran away meant that she understood clearly that she had done wrong.

This little girl was having many accidents—too many—because her fear that she might have even one accident made her tense and awkward in doing things.

The next time Margaret spilled her milk, her mother went into the other room and said to her cowering daughter, "Darling, we all have accidents. I have accidents too sometimes. But we can't let the milk just stay there on the floor. I will help you clean it up; we will do it together."

Margaret did not reply, because this is not what she had been experiencing recently. Without further discussion Mrs. Ward went back to the kitchen alone and cleaned up the spilled milk. But Margaret was aware of the fact that she had been neither scolded nor punished for what had happened.

It took time and much patience before Mother's new technique helped Margaret become a happy, trusting, cooperating, and responsible child.

What does discipline mean?

To begin with, let me give a helpful dictionary definition:

"Discipline is training that develops self-control, character, orderliness, and efficiency."

Discipline is not limited to correcting mistakes or wrongdoings. It is much more than that. It is all-inclusive, and always constructive. It is guided by love, affection, respect, and abides by clear rules.

Discipline is not something which is limited only to toilet training, mealtimes, getting a child to bed, or what to do when he doesn't hang his clothes on the hook. It is a basic ingredient in all of child-rearing. It must not be looked upon as something which makes parents mean or unfriendly. Quite the contrary; the understanding of discipline, combined with the ability to integrate it honestly into daily living, contributes greatly to the happy relationship between parents and their children. Discipline becomes a part of the child's personality and contributes to his social acceptance within the family, at school, and in the community. The patience, understanding, and time that you give your children so unhesitatingly every day are the very ingredients of the love which makes you a wonderful parent.

It is much easier for parents to discipline their children in the best possible way when they really know what they are doing and why. What they are doing is helping their child to gain self-control and confidence. Their goal for the child is self-control. As soon as he has gained it, he begins to discipline himself.

How can we help our child learn bladder control?

When you help your young child to learn bladder and bowel control you must be kind, gentle, and patient. You cannot help him learn such control by punishment because he then becomes tense and unhappy and this makes it impossible for him to function properly.

It is Mother who at first takes the entire responsibility for getting the child to the toilet regularly. As the child learns what is required of him and discovers that he can do it, he begins to assume the responsibility himself.

Each time the child is successful, he has a glorious sense of achievement. So does Mother—and how she deserves it for having brought her child so very far! Daddy shares in the congratulations. He is very proud.

The child's sense of achievement and the parents' approval and encouragement are powerful forces which help the young child to master everything that is involved—awareness of the body's demands, muscular control, handling of his own clothing, the ability to report an accident, and the ability to tear himself away from play or other fascinating activities to take care of his physical needs.

Some children learn quickly, some more slowly. All will have accidents and relapses. There is so very much to be learned!

When it is learned through sympathetic and encouraging guidance it is well and truly learned.

It is the constructive, not the fear–shame (inhibiting), kind of self-control and self-discipline that works wonders and makes happy children and happy parents.

Daytime training is usually much easier for the child than nighttime control. In order to experience the joy of a dry bed the child needs your help night after night. You will have to awaken him and take him to the bathroom. Be sure that he is sufficiently awake to realize what is happening. During this training period you will need to cut down his intake of liquids the last few hours before his bedtime.

The most important point about toilet training for you to remember is not to start it when the child is too young to understand and cooperate. There is no specific age in months or years when a child is ready to start this training. Before you start, discuss this with your pediatrician.

Once you have started toilet training with your child don't be impatient. Remember that it takes weeks rather than days and that some children respond quickly, others much more slowly.

Our boy usually forgets to wash before sitting at the table. What do you recommend?

The first time or two this happens, give him your reasons why he cannot do this, and then in a friendly but firm manner send him off to get washed before he sits down to the table. If he is too young to get sufficiently clean by himself you will have to help him. This is the training period in which you are the teacher. But slowly and consistently you start to relinquish the role of inspector and put more responsibility on him. A question of this sort: "Are you ready for dinner, Melvin?" before you call everyone else to the table will serve as a reminder to get washed. If Melvin appears at the table with dirty hands, a friendly remark like "What did you forget?" or "You hurried so fast but look what you forgot to do," will still make it his responsibility. After a few times, you will hear him saying: "Oops! Look what I forgot," and he will hurry off to the bathroom, wash, and return to the table as fast as he can.

There will be slip-backs of course. Melvin will quickly slide onto his chair, hiding his hands under the table, hoping that you will not see them. There will be days when he will claim that he has washed, even though all the evidence is to the contrary. On these occasions everyone will come out better if you are friendly but firm, without any emotional outburst. There can be no argument if you say: "A second washing with more soap is what you need." This type of statement gives him no alternative, but at the same time it does not ruin his status with the rest of the family. He knows full well that he did not get by with anything and will thus not try it too often. However, he will still test you out at various times, but this is a natural part of every growing child.

How can we teach our child to enjoy meal-times with us?

By making mealtimes happy times.

If Mother says to Alice: "Tell Daddy what you did today to the wall in your room," Alice immediately loses her appetite. So does Daddy, because he knows his daughter has done something wrong during the day and that *he* is now expected to do something about it. Mother in turn becomes further upset because Alice won't tell Daddy but just sits and stares at her plate, or because Daddy doesn't masterfully take charge. So nobody enjoys the meal that Mother spent so much time in preparing and has served so attractively.

Sometimes when a bright, lively child misbehaves frequently in the course of a busy and trying day, Mother may throw up her hands and cry, "Just wait till Daddy comes home!"

If Mother exercises a little self-control at this point, she can settle the matter more meaningfully and happily. If she acts hastily she may spank the child and feel that the problem has been taken care of. If this doesn't happen too frequently, parent and child can both quickly forgive and forget.

The brief squall is far better than the "Just wait till Daddy comes home!" If the child does have to wait, he endures long hours of inner torment. In waiting he may become very irritable indeed because he cannot bear the suspense. By the time Daddy comes and dinner is served, the child has no love for either.

When this sort of thing happens frequently, the child begins to associate mealtimes with unpleasantness. He may be late for meals because he does not want to come to the table. When he does come there may be all sorts of trouble, such as sulking and disturbing others in an effort to direct the parents' attention elsewhere.

If you think about it for a moment, you realize that when you are upset you do not enjoy your food. You dawdle over it; or you may eat very rapidly—and take pills for indigestion afterwards!

Good appetite and good eating habits do not go well together with meting out punishment. If punishment is to be discussed or inflicted, this should not take place just before or during mealtimes.

We do not punish our child, yet there is so much trouble with him at mealtimes. Why?

The reason can be one of a number. Here are a few:

1. The parents may be too vigilant and stern, ordering the child to sit up properly, take that elbow off the table, eat this with a fork and not with a spoon, and the other with a spoon and not a fork, hold the glass with both hands, and so on. No one can enjoy a meal when he is the constant target of commands and prohibitions, or when he knows he is under surveillance.

2. The grownups may be having dissensions at the table.

3. There may be open disagreement at the table about plans for the child's activities. If there is such disagreement, it should not be discussed at mealtimes—or at any other time when the child is present or can overhear. Present a genuinely united front to the child. About this you cannot pretend. He's got to know where he stands with each of you.

None of these possibilities may apply to you, but they are offered for you to consider and check off.

You may not be able to find the source of the trouble at all. But keep in mind that the best way to help your child build good eating habits is to see to it that mealtimes are happy times. When you do this you are helping not only your child but everyone at the table, including yourself.

This is as good a place as any for me to set down a curious discovery. A second-grade teacher got her class started on a discussion of habits. She soon discovered that to every one of a dozen pupils, *habits* meant *bad habits*. The fact that they felt so seemed to the teacher, and to me, rather revealing that good habits at home and in school are too often accepted and expected without praise or even discussion whereas bad habits are the cause of much nagging and repetition.

How can we teach our youngster good table manners?

Children are highly imitative. Good manners at the table are learned better by example than by lecturing about them.

It sometimes happens, however, that a problem develops even if the parents do have excellent manners.

I am thinking of my little friend Mickey, who used to gulp his food with such speed that he didn't pause or look up until he had finished. When he had lunch at the nursery school, the other children stared at him frequently, asking why he was in such a hurry to finish. He was being socially handicapped by his eating habits.

I discussed this with his parents. They were equally concerned because he had been doing this at home for some time.

This mother and father were highly intelligent and deeply interested in a wide variety of matters: the day's news, the stock market, politics and world affairs, the books they were reading, and psychology. They were keen, and one had to be on one's toes mentally to keep up with them.

Their love for their son was beautiful. How lucky Mickey was to have such parents!

These wonderful parents were fully aware how important it was for Mickey to eat well. While they talked at the table, each of them kept an eye on the boy and was reassured because he *was* eating well.

Too well. Mickey, of course, was getting his food down as fast as he could so that he could get away from the table as soon as possible. The table-talk was not for him; only the food. He could give no time or thought to manners.

As soon as the parents were aware of the situation they had little difficulty in changing their conversational habits so that the talk could include Mickey. At first, as usually happens, the boy did not fall in with the change. But they persevered, encouraging him to talk, asking sincere questions about his work and play, and helping him feel part of the family. They succeeded, and I shouldn't be at all surprised if the promising youngster soon begins to outtalk and outthink his parents.

Mickey's situation is not too unusual and serves to emphasize an important point:

Mealtimes are sociable occasions. When you have guests, or dine out, the talk includes everyone at table. You share not only food but ideas and experiences. This should be true as well when only the family is present.

Children from homes where they are made to feel "at home," that they *belong* and are part of a harmonious family, look forward to mealtimes, not only because they are hungry but also because they like the social atmosphere around the table. When they can participate in the exchange of ideas, the planning of future activities, and the family decisions made at the table, they have the feeling of being valuable and valued members of the family.

The old rule that children should be seen and not heard, and never speak unless spoken to, was once applied rigorously at mealtimes. In those days the dining room was very much like a classroom presided over by strict teachers (the parents). The children then had to learn the hard way, because the atmosphere was formal, cold, and forbidding—and correction was severe.

We marvel now at all the fun parents used to deny themselves in bringing up their children. And, looking back, many an adult can trace food dislikes, finicky tastes, small appetite, or a delicate digestion to the unrelaxed atmosphere that prevailed at the family table during his childhood.

A good rule to keep reminding yourself of is this: Your child is living his own full life while you are living yours. While you see him in the single dimension of a child, he sees himself as a complete person, with his own problems (that he may be working out by himself or with his friends). He is no more merely your baby than you are merely his mother—you are also a wife, a housekeeper, a shopper, member of the women's club, daughter of your own parents, a niece to some relatives and a cousin to others, and so on.

Look at your child every now and again—the table at mealtimes is a good time and place to do this—as a person whose day has been full of activities, and who should be encouraged to tell about himself even at the expense of the soup getting tepid. Lucky is the child who not only has plenty of calories to take aboard, but who feels that his parents find him and his doings interesting.

Our child demands all the attention and monopolizes all the conversation at mealtimes. What can we do?

It does sometimes seem difficult to keep the home life on an even keel. The child as young prima donna is a problem in every home.

You may have been leaning too far in encouraging your child to speak up, and have given him the feeling that mealtime is *his* time, that nobody else matters.

Bear in mind that discipline is not indulgence. It is guidance. Your child needs and wants your guidance. You are helping him not only to enjoy his food but to become a social being. This is important, because as he grows up he must go out into the world where people get along by give-and-take.

Mealtimes are the best times for the child to learn many things. He should learn to take his turn in listening as well as talking; to wait his turn for the food to be served; to pass a dish and to ask for one to be passed to him; to use spoon and knife and fork the way Mother and Daddy use them; to handle food without spilling it or throwing it about; to come to the table with hands and face washed, and hair combed; to ask to be excused when he has finished.

A child whose appetite is not large, or whose eating habits are not well established, may dawdle or "act up" in order to distract attention from the fact that he is not eating. This child must have his turn to talk, but he must also be made aware that the courses are not going to wait for him. When he is hungry between meals, tell him he can have food at the next mealtime. Your attitude should be kindly but firm, and soon eating the food that is served at dinner will be just as important as talking.

The child who persistently dawdles over his food needs to be served smaller portions and given a reasonable time limit. When the time is up, his plate should be removed pleasantly and without scolding. If he demands to keep it longer, it still must be taken away. Otherwise, he will continue to dawdle because he knows you don't mean it when you announce that he has five or ten minutes to finish.

If your child is monopolizing the conversation, another thing to try is to ask him a question. A question always makes one pause to think. When he replies, the opportunity is presented for you to remark what So-and-So (somebody known to all) did or said in a similar situation, or what you think about it. The conversation then becomes more general.

The child whose talk is taken seriously, and who is directed toward taking himself seriously, is not going to be "acting up" for long.

Sunday breakfast is a wonderful time in most families. Daddy is home and glad to be home, and Daddy often takes a hand in preparing this breakfast. Sometimes the children and Daddy prepare and serve the whole meal, giving Mother a grand surprise, or at least a rest.

I remember Bennet. Every Monday morning when he arrived at school he always greeted me with "Guess what Daddy made for breakfast yesterday." At that time Bennet's great ambition was to be a daddy so that he could make Sunday breakfast for the family.

Mealtime is neither exclusively adult nor child time. It is family time.

✳✦❀✦✳✦❀✦✳✦❀✦✳✦❀✦✳✦❀

SIX

Do you enjoy your child?
Does he enjoy you?

✳✦❀✦✳✦❀✦✳✦❀✦✳✦❀✦✳✦❀

Why can't we have fun together?

Having fun together is a very important ingredient in the magic of bringing up your child.

Little Stephen, working with his mother in the garden, suddenly looked up at her with a very long face. "Why—why can't we have fun together the way Tommy and his mother do?" he blurted out.

Stephen's mother could hardly believe her ears. She decided it was a case of the grass in the next yard looking greener. All the same she began to cast her eye and tune her ear for what went on in that yard next door.

The lesson she learned was at first bitter to swallow.

It was hard for her to accept the fact which was plain as could be—that shouts of laughter came over the fence, and that Tommy and his mother *were* having fun together, and that Tommy's mother was not harming her child by having fun with him.

It took courage for Stephen's mother to compare her situation with the one next door. She began to realize that she had become so serious about providing a good home for her son that she had forgotten the important ingredient—enjoyment, the light touch.

She could not exactly copy Tommy's mother, who happened to be one of those agile, girlish women to whom active play comes naturally. But Stephen's mother did find that she could have fun with her child in her own way. She discovered that behind everything she had been doing with and for Stephen was an attitude of duty and self-sacrifice. When she began to enjoy doing things with him and for him, she solved her problem.

Here is another case, that of Rachel, age seven, begging her mother not to send her to the circus with Daddy. The mother is naturally alarmed. Surely there is something very wrong with a child who doesn't want to go to the circus. Rachel quickly retreats into the child's refuge of "No. I won't go! I don't want to. I won't!"

Rachel couldn't explain, yet she had actually made it clear. But Mother had closed her ears. She couldn't believe that Rachel didn't want to go *with Daddy!*

The truth was that whenever Daddy took Rachel out it was because he felt he should, in order to let his wife have a rest. Because he considered these outings a duty, he was bored to begin with and easily irritated, so he always brought back a sobbing, or at any rate miserable, Rachel. It had not occurred to him that he could actually enjoy himself with his little daughter.

A mother who goes about her daily work grimly— or with bitterness, resentment, or constant complaint—is only making things harder for herself. She is making her home an unpleasant place to be in, and her child will have to find his fun outside. When that happens he does not always find the right kind of fun.

A father who comes home looking as if the weight of the world were on his shoulders, who grouses, and snaps when spoken to, is not only a Santa Claus in reverse, but also a man with a load of joylessness. He is communicating to his child fear of an outside world that does such things to Daddy.

Just imagine how it is for the child whose mother and father are both cheerless. His home is unpleasant, he is uneasy in it, and the outside world is to be feared. For such a child, life is just a thing that has to be endured.

Some husbands and wives carry on a feud with each other which has become so much a part of their life together that they're no longer even aware of it. I know a mother who boasted that she and her husband never quarreled in their child's presence. "In fact, John and I never quarrel at all!" she added proudly.

Her mother-in-law, who loved her but loved the unhappy grandchild even more, said sadly, "There is a way of quarreling without words."

She was right. Silent reproach, anger, and tension are often louder than words. So are sarcasms, even mild ones. There is a way of playful "needling" which is a kind of disguised fault-finding. If there are hostile feelings, it is better for the life of the family to have them out and clear the air, rather than to carry on a feud. But not in the child's presence.

When a teacher or someone else professionally trained in the field of child development visits your home, this expert can rather quickly detect the atmosphere of family living. Since the visitor is not emotionally a part of it, he can be objective. Let him help you, if you feel the need of it. This kind of help can be a short cut for you to a better and easier way of life. But you can accept such help only if you really want it and fully understand that it is not offered as criticism of you, any more than the doctor's advice on health is criticism.

Many parents can accept such help. Many others cannot.

However, it is possible for you to help yourself. Just sit back and think things over. Ask this question: "Am I enjoying our child, my husband, our home—and myself?"

Since we are all human, we are certain to have disagreements, and sometimes to quarrel. We are sometimes depressed. We are sometimes worried—about job, illness in the family, money, the future, and at times about nothing that we can definitely pin down. We are sometimes annoyed; sometimes we feel exhausted.

Life has its ups and downs, and I certainly don't

mean to suggest that you can make it all ups and no downs by putting on a Pollyanna air. That's no fun either, and the child senses what's underneath.

On the other hand, having fun does not mean that you must or should be trying to play, laugh, and romp all day long. Just try that, and in no time at all you'll find yourself and your child worn out.

It comes down to this—

One: When parents let gloom, anxiety, or any other variety of joylessness become a basic attitude, and thus an atmosphere that pervades the home and all its activities, they miss a great deal of life. Even so, it is their child who suffers most, because this is the atmosphere he has to grow up in, and because it will affect him, in one way or another, the rest of his days.

Two: Family fun is the result of an attitude that creates a pleasant home atmosphere. In such a warm, sunny "climate," laughter and good feeling well up naturally and often.

Three: Before a child can have fun with other children, he must experience fun with his parents.

Is it important that we play with our child?

Yes. Through play a baby begins to try out his body and to learn about the marvelous things he can do with it. When he plays with his fingers and toes he is learning about them. When he plays with his rattle, he is discovering that objects can do things (it makes a funny noise), and that he can do things with objects (he can bang it, throw it).

It is all wonderful, and wonder is at the bottom of delight and laughter.

Mother and Daddy find the same wonder and delight in playing with their baby, taking note of his responses and discoveries—and so play begins naturally in the family.

When the parents play with their baby, they learn too. They see how his ability to manipulate things and himself increases. There is a thrill in watching the growth of your own child, and another in helping that growth and having a part in it. Meantime the baby is learning the important fact that the best fun is the fun that is shared, and he very quickly responds to the fun kind of laughter.

The fun kind is the laughing together. There is another kind—being laughed *at*. That isn't fun—at least not for the one being laughed at.

In the beginning Mother coos, sings, and talks to her baby when she bathes and changes and feeds him. To the small child bathing and feeding are pleasant in themselves. Mother's smiling and laughing deepens the pleasure. Then Mother claps the baby's hands in pattycake or counts on his fingers and toes, "This little piggy went to market." She tries peekaboo, shows him byebye, or gives him her fingers to help pull him up into the great adventure of sitting or standing.

All this is play and learning for the child, and it is play and teaching for the parent.

How can I get all my housework done and play with my boy too?

This can be a problem for mothers, a big everyday problem. For many years I wondered why some mothers managed so much better than others. Were they gifted with some special talent?

Yes, they do have a special talent, a sort of parental "green thumb." However, it is not so special that others can't develop it also.

The secret lies in our own minds, in what we feel about work as opposed to play.

There was a time when play was frowned upon as frivolous. It was thought of as a distraction and an attempt to escape from the stern duties of life. Now we know that play is a form of learning, exploring, discovering, and piling up of useful experiences.

We still divide work from play, but the dividing line has become blurred. When you enjoy your work, you have fun doing it, and this is not far from the kind of fun you have in play. You also find that work comes easier and is better done when you do enjoy it. Work enjoyed is fun with a serious purpose.

And, when you enjoy your work, your child can grow into that enjoyment.

The growing child begins to distinguish work from play. Work is what Mother is doing in the kitchen, bedroom, or wherever. He loves to be with Mother, where things are going on that he can observe or be part of. How can he understand that when he gets into it he interferes and makes a mess and more work for her?

He can't. It will take him a long time to arrive at this understanding. Meantime, he's just got to do things. How else can he learn?

Mother should, whenever she can, have her child near while she works, giving him something to play with by himself in his high chair or play pen. She can explain what she is doing as she goes along. It will make sense to him—not necessarily in the way of comprehension but at least of feeling that he is in on whatever is going on. Singing or humming to herself—and to him—has the same effect.

Sooner or later he will do something to get in the way of his mother's work. He drops his toy or throws it and waits for Mother to pick it up. Or he begins to cry when she leaves the room and she has to run back to make sure he's all right. Or he does so much banging that Mother feels she can't stand it another minute. This is the time to take him away quietly and pleasantly. Have his favorite toys within reach, and turn the radio or record player on softly.

He will probably cry even so, because he still wants to be with you. But since violent emotion has not been aroused in him by the emotion in yourself, he will stop fairly soon. He can play quietly by himself, and with great absorption. He does not really have to have you around all the time. But he does want and need you around just enough of the time, for him (and this varies with each child), so that he doesn't feel alone in the world.

The tot who can often be with his mother while she works, and who has pleasant feelings about that work, soon wants to participate in it—because it is fun, play, sharing, being part of the family, and learning to do more and more things. Work, play, and fun then get mixed up very happily.

Day-in-and-day-out fun, even while planning dinner, washing dishes, readying the laundry, and emptying the wastebaskets—this is the ideal, and worth striving for. Play can become a part of it. Little games suddenly emerge, created by child or mother, often in collaboration. This is the happiest way for a child to learn that work means getting things done.

It is only slowly that the child begins to see the whole of any one operation or task, instead of small, separate parts of it. Only then does he begin to understand the serious purpose behind the bustle and the homely, friendly noises of getting things done.

Even before he learns this, however, he begins to sense somehow that work is important. And he loves to help, because then *he* feels important, too.

That is a wonderful feeling. The child who experiences it—all children do, given the chance—has grown from play as play into enjoyment of work. He has developed the grown-up wish, will, and ability to be helpful.

He'll soon get over that, so far as household chores are concerned. All the same, Mother can congratulate herself for having brought herself and her child through a difficult stage with a minimum of discomfort and a maximum of profit. Which means a maximum of fun.

How can we show our child that we enjoy his company?

By being interested in him and spending time with him.

Do you really enjoy your child's company? Or do you find yourself too often saying, "Leave me alone and go out and play," or "I'm busy; go look at television"?

When I see parents and their children tackling problems together, it is to me one of the most genuine signs of love and affection. It means that the child knows, and lives with the happy assurance, that he can bring his problems to his mother and father. They may not be able to clear up every difficulty, but they will do their best.

Give yourself time with your children—time to know them, time to talk and to listen, time to help them. Give your children the feeling that when they need and want you, you have the time for them no matter how busy you are. Respect your child and in turn he will respect and enjoy you.

Mrs. Purcell told me about an incident that made a deep and lasting impression upon her. The Purcells have a five-year-old girl, Candis, and a boy, Peter, two years. The parents would go out occasionally, leaving a baby sitter with the children. The week before Thanksgiving was especially heavy with social engagements and the Purcells left the children with baby sitters who were excellent and of whom the children were fond. The morning after the third night out, when Candis' mother came into her room, Candis asked, "Did you and Daddy have a nice time last night?"

"Yes, thank you," Mrs. Purcell replied.

After a pause, Candis added, "I hope you and Daddy are not going out again tonight. Peter and I have had three different baby sitters. Don't you think three times a week is a lot of times to leave us alone?"

Mrs. Purcell was completely caught off guard, but she answered, "Candy, you are absolutely right. Daddy and I have been out a lot this week, but it was a very busy week for us. Three of our friends all wanted us over to dinner. That was very nice of them, don't you think?"

"Yes," Candy replied, "but Peter and I love you too."

As Mrs. Purcell related this experience I could see that she was surprised at her daughter's expression and delighted that Candis had enough confidence in her to state her feeling so forthrightly.

You should never underestimate the ability of a young child to analyze a situation which concerns him. Here was a situation in which a child was telling her parents how much she enjoys their company. At the same time she was indicating to them her need for reassurance of their love and companionship and her feeling of belonging.

Our daughter uses bathtime as funtime. Is this a good idea?

Bathtime is a wonderful time for you and your child to enjoy each other. She will want to splash around and play with her washcloth and soap. If the soap floats there is no danger of its going to the bottom of the tub and the child slipping on it. There are also cakes of soap on a cord which can be put around the child's neck and which protect him from such an accident.

Be sure that you are appropriately dressed for bathtub fun because you will undoubtedly get splashed. Fun at this time does not mean overexcitement, nor does it necessitate messing up the bathroom.

Young children especially love the "making of rain" in the bathtub. Ask your child to close his eyes or put his hands over them while you drip the washcloth over his head. Making it rain on you as well is enjoyment to the full for him so let him drip some water on your arm.

Of course, every bath cannot be a long playful time. But at least a couple of times a week it can be one of the happiest times of the day for both of you. Your child will respond with glee and delight. You will reciprocate with enthusiasm. Don't be surprised if your child doesn't want to get out of the tub.

When our four-year-old is housebound, she frequently asks, "What can I do now, Mommy?"

The indoor day is the best kind of day for you to help your child become resourceful, to exercise his imagination, to create. Since there are going to be such days, have small projects ready in reserve which you can work on and enjoy together. Here are some suggestions:

Make a blue denim or unbleached muslin scrapbook. You do the sewing and your child cuts and pastes in the pictures.

Make a sock doll from an old pair of socks, letting your child stuff it with cotton batting. See if he can come up with suggestions about how the hair and face should be done.

Make a tambourine from two paper plates, sewing little bells around the edge, and let your child make a picture with crayons or paints on each of the plates.

Make doll hats from paper cups.

Make hats, puppets, or masks from paper bags.

Make dolls or animals from pipe cleaners and clothespins. (By the way, it is a good idea to lay in a supply of pipe cleaners. They are inexpensive, available at any toy store or drug counter, take up little space, and are almost limitless in their use.)

Make cars, trains, trucks, or houses out of milk cartons.

Make hats and boats out of newspaper or wrapping paper.

Have a botany project—small plants to be replanted in another pot, trimmed, watered, and given to your child to be taken care of as his very own. Sweet potatoes, carrots, flower bulbs, and pumpkin seeds grow quickly and are fun to watch. Cut off the end of a sweet potato and place it, cut side down, in a jar of water. Add water now and then and you'll soon have a beautiful vine. The same can be done with a carrot top. Let your child try it. Such "gardening" delights a child, especially a town or city child. It is creative magic to him.

Children are ingenious at making or helping to make all kinds of bells. At times, they enjoy just ringing the bell alone. At other times, they prefer ringing the bell to the accompaniment of music. Small flowerpots, discarded Jello molds, tin cans, paper cups, small cardboard boxes, and many more such things, can be combined with pipe cleaners, small sticks, and the like, to make bells for children to ring, or rattles for them to shake. Children like to search around for something to use for a clapper inside the bell. Sandpaper tacked to small wooden blocks, or to small cardboard boxes, gives them additional opportunity for making rhythmical sounds.

Once your child sees that such things can be done, he will be doing them, and trying out other things he thinks up by himself or with visiting playmates. You don't want the children to be using or destroying articles you need, so it is a good idea to have a "treasure bag" filled with discarded odds and ends. The children will find more things to do with bits of rope, yarn, string, buttons, scraps of material, and what-not.

Resourcefulness, as it becomes a part of the child's everyday living, means looking through the materials at hand not only to invent or create something, but to make do when what he happens to need is not at hand. If, for example, he needs paste, show him how to mix flour and water to make it. If he wants to paint and has mislaid his brush, don't make him put his paints away. Instead, fold a pipe cleaner in half and let him dip the folded end into the paint as a substitute brush. It will make different and interesting effects. If you have no pipe cleaners, wrap a small swab of cotton tightly around a pencil or a flat stick from an ice cream bar. He will enjoy painting with these. They are new to him and thus experimental. Later when he finds his paintbrush, he will use it with renewed enthusiasm.

Resourcefulness should be encouraged at all times. It helps to build a better sense of values and is a characteristic that will serve your child well the rest of his life.

When and how should we introduce our child to music?

Music is a source of relaxation, enrichment, and happiness, even to an infant. The more you sing and hum to your baby, the more he enjoys it; and if he could speak he would probably say: "I want more." In addition to the songs you sing to him, let him listen to music on the radio and on records. Keep the volume of the radio and record player low, so that the music does not blare and frighten him.

As your child grows older, he may want to sing with you, as well as by himself. Encourage him as much as you can, but don't force him. At all times music must be a pleasant experience. Never force your child to perform in front of guests, no matter how proud you might be of his ability to sing or play an instrument. This can embarrass him deeply. Many children deliberately show little interest in music because their parents have insisted upon showing them off to relatives and friends.

Singing in a group is lots of fun, particularly in a family group. Singing together at home in the evening is something most children would look forward to enthusiastically, and I heartily recommend it. Singing while working together, whether it is washing dishes or cleaning the house, with each member joining in, makes the work go much faster. Take turns in singing solo parts, with the whole group joining in on the chorus. It is always good group fun. It also helps to ease friction that might start from time to time between members of a family; and it adds to harmonious relationships.

Records give children much pleasure. They can listen for hours at a time. There is an overwhelming quantity of children's records available today, and you have to be selective in order to find those which your child will enjoy hearing again and again. You will get to know his likes and dislikes. There are lullabies, ranch songs, Mother Goose songs, music without words, including symphonies written for children, folk songs, rhythmic tunes, and many others.

At times a child likes to just sit and listen to these records. Or he will dance, clap, or jump, and love every minute of it. There will be times when he will invite you to dance with him. Conversely, he may become very self-conscious if you come in and watch what he is doing.

A child will have his favorite record or records and he will play them over and over and over. He will do this while he is looking at his books, playing with toys, or just listening with pleasure. You will wonder how long you can stand it, but if you ask the child to keep the volume low, it won't bother you.

Television frequently offers a rich variety of music for children. This enables a child to watch what other people do with the music. Later, or on another day, he may do the very thing that he saw the people on television do with the music. For example, he watches someone do a dance, and he may dance; or he may play with hand puppets. Even if he doesn't have a record of this music, he simply sings or hums the tune, and enjoys himself completely.

When your child is seven or eight years old, you will think about music lessons for him. And like most parents, you will probably think about introducing your child to the piano. In order to learn to play a musical instrument, however, a child must have the interest and desire to do it. He must understand why he has to practice. Many children practice the piano day after day, but their hearts are not in it. They do not enjoy it, and they make no headway with it. This is not only expensive to parents in terms of money, but it is costly to the child because he has learned laboriously to dislike the instrument, as well as the music he has been trying to play.

We want children to learn to play the musical instrument of their choice because it can give them many hours of pleasure during childhood, and in adulthood as well. I know many fathers who come home after a day of hard work and forget all about their problems by playing the piano, organ, accordion, or some other instrument. They lose themselves completely in the music, and find it is restful and relaxing and creative.

Don't try to make a professional musician out of your child unless he shows superior talent and has a very special interest in music. Let him enjoy music for what he gets out of it.

My husband can't spend much time with our son because of his job schedule. What can he do about it?

After a full day's work at the office, a father is often tired and perhaps worried about one thing or another.

He may not feel up to going outdoors and playing with his son. But during the week end, it is almost always possible for him to arrange his schedule to include play or some kind of activity. It will go a long way in cementing the father–son relationship.

One of the most heartwarming stories I have ever heard was related by Milton Gross, the sports columnist. He was talking about Ray Robinson, who won the middleweight boxing championship of the world five times.*

When Ray Robinson and his wife returned from a trip to Paris they brought their son a hand-carved toy which the child cherished. He displayed it prominently in his room and often he would play with it by the hour.

Recently, however, Ray's wife, Edna Mae, noticed the toy was missing from its usual place. She asked the child about it. He said he had given it to a neighborhood friend.

"You liked it so much," Mrs. Robinson said to her eight-year-old son. "Why did you give it away?"

"Now," the child said, "he lets me play ball on his team."

That night when her husband came home, Edna Mae asked Ray Jr. to repeat the story to his father.

"I had to give him something, Dad," the child said. "I don't get a chance to play on the team with the other kids because I don't play well."

"What do you think of that?" Edna Mae asked.

"Here's a child whose father is one of the greatest ath-

* Reprinted by permission of New York *Post.* Copyright © 1958 New York Post Corporation.

letes in the world and his son must bribe another child to be able to play."

"Honey," Ray Robinson said, "it's not going to happen again. I've been busy, but it looks like I've been too busy for my own boy. That's not what I've been fighting for."

The next day he called for his son at school at 3 o'clock. "How about a game of ball?" he asked.

"Can I ask the other kids, Dad?" Ray Jr. said.

"Sure," his father replied. "Get the other kids and I'll umpire the game."

I called Ray Robinson at his home. I wanted to know about his plans for defending his middleweight title. Edna Mae answered the phone.

"My husband's out back on the lot umpiring a ball game," Edna Mae said.

"Can he come to the phone?" I asked.

"Not for anything," Edna Mae said. "He's having more fun than he's ever had in his life. He'll call you later."

That evening Ray Robinson phoned me. "I got a story for you," he said.

I wondered if he would tell me about his next fight. Instead he told me about the game.

"There was a tough play at home," he said. "It could have been called either way. I thought my boy was out and I called it that way.

"Ray Jr. jumps up and he sticks his face right close to mine. 'Oh, gee, Dad,' he says, 'I think Carmen Basilio [whom Robinson had fought a short time before] must have hit you too hard.'"

Over the phone Robinson laughed so heartily he broke into a cough. There was undiluted joy in the laughter. It was so unlike the Ray Robinson I had known. "I never realized," he said, "how important it was to my boy to be close to him. I never realized how important it was to me to be close to my boy."

"Is this something new?" I asked.

"For the first time in my life," he said, "I'm really enjoying myself. For the first time I'm not running after something.

"Do you know something," he said over the phone, "being a champion's been part of my life, but being a father's a bigger part. I thought I had everything when I won the title again the fifth time, but when my boy gave his toys away so he could play with the other kids I realized I didn't have much."

If fathers don't like to play baseball there are many other activities that their children would like to do with them. It is not only because other children's parents play with them that makes your child want you to play with him. It is also because he needs and wants your companionship. He needs to learn fair play and good sportsmanship from you, and in addition he wants to think of you as his best friend as well as his parent. He can attain all this if you do work and play with him. If you can do this for only ten minutes a day, more if possible, these periods together will provide some of the most valuable and precious experiences that both of you will have.

My husband brings home gifts for our child every time he returns from a trip. Is this wise?

One of the common ways in which we show our affection is by giving, but gift-giving can be overdone. If Daddy always comes home from his trips with presents tucked under his arm or hiding in his briefcase, your child not only expects the gift each time—he may actually become more interested in getting it than in seeing Daddy. If Daddy fails to bring home a gift one time the child will be keenly disappointed and may cry, and Daddy, who is unprepared for this reaction, will suddenly realize that the gift has become more important to his child than he has.

Some parents who spend little time with their child believe they can compensate for this lack of attention by plying him with too many gifts too often. This does more harm than good because it indicates to the child that in his parents' eyes material things are more important than love and affection and time together.

There is another form of giving that can be harmful. That is "giving way." It is indulgence when you give your child what he wants for no other reason than that you love him and he wants it.

The child who gets what he wants whenever he wants it is being given to understand that his wishes are law. Behind such indulgence is the kind of love that usually produces the "spoiled" child—a person unpleasant to others because he is always demanding, and unpleasant to himself because he actually suffers when he cannot get what he wants in later life. And of course no child can count on his future world treating him the way his indulgent mother or father did.

Neither gifts nor indulgence—giving or giving way —can be substituted for companionship and guidance.

Do we hurt our son's feelings when we laugh at him?

There will be times when your child, without realizing it, is going to say or do something that is irresistibly funny, and you have to laugh. If it is laughter at his expense, give him a hug while you are laughing. Often you cannot explain to him, because what he has done or said is comical only from a grown-up point of view. Indeed, it is not necessary to explain. If your laughter is without ridicule, the child knows it. He knows he is being appreciated, not humiliated. And he is delighted with his surprising ability to make people laugh. He shows his appreciation by laughing himself, enthusiastically. It is a new magic, and he is going to try it out again and again.

If he is not pleased, don't feel that your child has

no sense of humor. Accept the fact that his sense of humor is not the same as yours, or is in an early stage of development. But if he looks hurt, you can be certain that even though you did not intend it, there is ridicule in your laughter. Apologize as best you can, for you have hurt him in a way that no one should be hurt.

"*You don't love me!*" *Why does our child say this?*

Because their small daughter sometimes cried out, "You don't love me!" Mr. and Mrs. Desmond brought this question to me, and I am glad that they did. Most parents simply assume that their child knows they love him. Shocking though it may be to you, this is not always true.

The child has to live in an adult world. He is being taught to conform, and is being disciplined when he forgets some of the countless do's and don't's, or makes mistakes, or has accidents. Isn't it natural that he should now and then have frightening doubts that you love him?

You are providing him with food, shelter, and clothing, and the care necessary to his health. But this is not enough. Members of a family are united by strong emotional ties. Sometimes they seem more disunited than united, but even so they give and take and share—both emotionally and physically. If this were not true, homes wouldn't be anything more than boarding houses!

When your love for your child is not only strong but understanding and constructive, you give him a sense of security which is tremendously important to him throughout life. This sense of security is very much like the feeling of having solid ground under one's feet. Fears, troubles, and problems are more easily faced and cleared up.

There are many different ways to express your love to your child. No two parents show their feelings in the same way. You best know the ways that are most meaningful and satisfying to you and your child.

Though the words are important, telling your child that you love him is not sufficient. You have to show that you mean what you say. Kissing, hugging, petting, clowning, playing, singing, laughing, and praising when praise is deserved, help a great deal to give the child the feeling that he is loved. One of the most genuine signs of love and affection between parents and children is that of solving problems together.

Whatever variety or combination of techniques or ways of expressing your love and affection to your children you use, just be sure that they add up to telling your child "We love you!"

⤙☙⤚⤙☙⤚*⤙☙⤚*⤙☙⤚*⤙☙

SEVEN

Growing child, growing parents

⤙☙⤚⤙☙⤚*⤙☙⤚*⤙☙⤚*⤙☙

How can we know what to expect of our child?

There are many books with charts, based on scientific studies, that give you an idea of what to expect in the way of a child's development from year to year. They are helpful but are not meant to be absolute. You will learn at what age many children walk, talk, count, and so on. But if your own child is not acting by the chart, do not worry. He is himself, not anything in a table of statistics.

Chart-minded parents often find that they themselves are human in a way not covered by any chart, whether for children or adults.

This is illustrated by my friends the Pruits on their

daughter Barbara's first birthday. Grandparents and other relatives had been invited. Mrs. Pruit made a beautiful birthday cake. The lighted candle on the cake pleased Barbara, and when everyone sang "Happy Birthday to You," she laughed with great delight. But when she was served her piece of the cake, she wouldn't eat it; she only played with the frosting, and her mother was disappointed.

Mr. Pruit was also disappointed, but for another reason. He had planned a big surprise for Barbara and hadn't even told his wife about it. When dinner was over, he brought in his birthday present for Barbara. She stared at it, and then went off in the opposite direction. Her mother gasped at her lack of enthusiasm and her father was completely crushed.

Then, suddenly, the Pruits began to laugh, and so did their guests. The Pruits had been expecting their one-year-old to enjoy and appreciate things entirely beyond her comprehension and experience. She could not possibly have eaten a piece of birthday cake. Even less could she have been expected to appreciate and love her birthday present—a tricycle!

To go back to the question. My answer is: The best thing to expect is—the unexpected!

Mr. Carter took four-year-old Arthur to a farm to see some baby chickens. It was fun for both of them. Arthur asked the farmer many questions about where the little chicks came from. On the way home, Arthur and his father talked about how the hen sat on the eggs and how the chicks came out of the shells. At home,

Arthur told his mother all about it at the dinner table. Mr. and Mrs. Carter were very pleased with the success of their experiment. They felt that the trip to the farm had been an excellent educational experience for their son.

About an hour after dinner, the Carters missed Arthur, who usually played in the living room at that time. Mrs. Carter went to look for him. She found him sitting on the kitchen floor. He looked up as she approached and motioned for her to walk quietly. She stooped, and he whispered in her ear, "I am sitting on three eggs for the chickens to hatch."

Mrs. Carter was so startled that she quickly went to get her husband. Together they convinced Arthur that there would be no chickens, persuaded him to get up, and helped him to clean the mess of broken eggs off the floor and himself. Arthur was sadly disappointed that he could not produce baby chicks by sitting on eggs.

The Carters came to me the next morning, deeply concerned. Mr. Carter was afraid that his son was retarded, abnormally slow, because he didn't understand the difference between humans and hens. Mrs. Carter was more concerned over the fact that until she had helped Arthur up from the floor, he apparently hadn't realized that he had broken the eggs.

We talked for two hours before these parents were convinced that Arthur was a bright child and that his misunderstanding was natural. He had loved the fluffy chicks and had wanted some for himself. So he had gone to work with deep concentration and a feeling of important responsibility—to hatch some eggs.

As the Carters were leaving, Mrs. Carter said, almost to herself, "I wonder how it feels to sit on eggs. . . ."

I replied, "I've never sat on eggs, so I don't know. But I'm sure that whatever it felt like to Arthur, he assumed that this was the way it felt to a hen."

Then we laughed!

Throughout childhood, there are usually more joys and laughter for parents than there are worries. True, there is the time Andy decides he won't eat, and throws his plate to the floor. And the time Carolyn washes Mother's cashmere sweater in the toilet bowl, to be helpful. And the time. . . .

Well, remember to laugh—later if you can't laugh now. A sense of humor gives perspective and helps you grow in depth while your child is growing in all directions.

A parent's life is certainly never dull. There are plenty of mountains and valleys but few plateaus. When you do hit a plateau, stretch, remember, laugh—and get ready for the next surprise.

Why does our child sometimes act like a baby one day and a grownup the next?

In Chapter Two, "Suddenly a Child," I answered a similar question about the toddler.

Children may make a sudden leap in some direction,

and then sometimes revert to earlier—even infantile—behavior before going on again. The slip-back may be in quite another field from the one in which they've progressed.

In dressing, for example, the two-year-old tells you, in no uncertain terms, "I want to do it"—meaning that he does not want your help in putting his arms into the sleeves of his sweater and his legs into his overalls. Many four-year-olds are entirely independent in dressing.

But here is five-year-old Ernie, who has been independent in this way for a long time. Now he is asking for help, whining that he can't dress himself. Why?

Since he has to get in and out of clothes so many times a day, is he bored and tired of the whole thing? He may be. But it is possible that for some reason unknown to his parents or himself he has gone back to the young child's helpless dependence.

He won't be doing this long if you don't make an issue of it. Encourage him. Help him. He'll be off again soon on his own.

Children of any age surprise their parents by what seems to be a slip-back which is only an unexpected reminder of immaturity. If parents have been going along thinking their child is all grown up when his age itself tells them he cannot be, they may have a shock.

I recall the look of horror on a father's face when he told me what had occurred the night before. He was still visibly shaken when he talked about it.

Several hours after dinner, when it was getting dark, he had gone out to look for his eleven-year-old daughter

Ellen. He called her but there was no reply. He walked around the block, and started back through the alley behind their house. He found her there in the alley with her friend Marilyn. They were looking through a garbage can for—they had said—something good to eat!

To Mr. McLean, Ellen's father, this was a terrible thing. He could not understand it. Both girls were from well-to-do families and had been given almost everything that they wanted. Ellen had eaten a good dinner and could not possibly have been so hungry as to be driven to going through garbage in search of food. If she was hungry, she had only to ask at home. Was it possible that Ellen, at eleven, didn't understand the difference between clean food and garbage? If she had done such a thing at four or five, he might have been less concerned. But Ellen was now so neat and clean about everything, and had developed such a good sense of values. How could she be so confused about this!

Mr. McLean was afraid that this might be the beginning of something serious. Was his daughter going to be a delinquent? Or was what she had done a symptom of abnormality?

He and his wife had asked an explanation from Ellen, but she seemed not to have one. This had worried them even more. They felt that she was holding back something. They hadn't slept at all that night.

It took hours to reassure this father that his daughter was not on the road to ruin, and that he and his wife had not failed as parents.

There was no use now trying to get any kind of

explanation from Ellen, who must have been frightened and embarrassed by her parents' attitude. I asked Mr. McLean to forget the whole thing. Ellen had suffered sufficient embarrassment. I reminded him that however grown-up she might appear, she was still more child than adult. The fact that the mother and father had successfully and happily brought their daughter through the first eleven years of her life did not mean that their job was completed, and that their daughter would sail through her teens easily. She must still be helped and guided.

This father did not realize that hurt pride had loomed large behind his great disturbance. It had made him lose perspective. The very thought of his daughter looking for cast-off food in a refuse can was to him extremely humiliating. He said he was afraid some of the neighbors might have seen her. He didn't even want to talk to Marilyn's parents about the incident.

Two years later I met Ellen, and her father and mother, on the day of her graduation from grade school. They were a happy, proud, and loving trio. I am sure they had entirely forgotten the garbage incident.

Why does our son say "I can't" when he really can?

Here are some of the more common reasons:

1. There may be a brief reversion, a slip-back to

younger behavior, as with Ernie who could dress himself but suddenly demanded help, saying "I can't."

2. When a child is afraid he may not be able to do a certain thing in front of others, even though he knows he can do it when he is alone, he often says "I can't."

3. When you ask a child to do something he doesn't want to do, he sometimes says "I can't" in the hope that this will save him from having to do it.

4. The shy child frequently says "I can't." Shyness is a kind of double embarrassment. He is embarrassed not only by being called upon, but at being unable to respond.

5. The child who is exploited by his parents to show off at the piano, sing, recite, or dance, sometimes says "I can't," which means "Please don't make me do it."

If your own child is saying "I can't" when you know he can and wants to, help him so that he has the feeling of accomplishment. But if you are sure he is saying it just to get out of doing something, be friendly but firm in seeking his cooperation in getting the job done.

Our daughter says she doesn't want to grow up, that she prefers to stay a little girl. What makes her feel this way?

Children have many ways of indicating to you that something is wrong.

Susan, for example, was being told frequently by her parents that when she grew up she would have to learn this and that and work hard at many new things. Behind such teaching and disciplining was the attitude: "You're going to have to do it when you grow up, so you had better learn right now." As a result, Susan was not looking forward to the future with pleasure or anticipation. She was beginning to dread growing up.

More than this was involved, however. Susan's mother, in guiding her daughter, had the habit of saying, "If you do this again, I won't love you any more." Occasionally when Mother was having a difficult day, she would say, "Daddy won't love you when he comes home because you have been a naughty girl."

Susan drew the conclusion that if she remained little —just being "good" and not trying out anything new —there would be less danger of losing the love of Mother and Daddy. To grow up meant doing all kinds of things, and when she tried and made mistakes, she was told that Mother and Daddy wouldn't love her any more if she failed again.

No wonder Susan was confused. She really didn't want to grow up.

Have you ever heard a parent say to his child, "If you do that, I won't love you?" Even if it is said in jest, such a remark is frightening to a child. No parent means to carry out this threat, so he should never say it. Never, in word or in deed, withdraw or threaten to withdraw your love from your child.

Our child takes everything for granted. Why is he so unappreciative of what we do for him?

Often Mother and Father buy things for their child because they want him to have them. But if the child does not feel the need for these things, he cannot show appreciation or even pretend to be interested in them.

You do many things for your child that he does not understand well enough to appreciate. If, for example, you have opened a savings account for him for his future college education, you can hardly expect him to be grateful. It is only when he is ready to enter college that he will understand fully what you have done for him.

A child's gratitude is honest, genuine. There is no self-awareness or calculation mixed up in it. It is only as he grows older that he learns to show a pretended enthusiasm or gratitude. He may learn to do this only because he knows it will please you, and may lead to your getting something else for him—something he really wants.

This is not a good way to learn to be appreciative. On this road lies wheedling, intriguing, and all that kind of insincerity.

In time, your child is bound to learn how to be politely enthusiastic and appreciative, because it is socially expected in life; without it he would be socially handicapped. But you don't want him to feel forced to pretend —not with you.

You do things for your child happily, because you like to. Your reward is growing up with him, sharing and enjoying with him, watching him develop under your guidance and companionship into a fine person.

If you are demanding expressed gratitude for this, you are asking for more than the immature child mind is able to give. And, in demanding it, are you really loving? Your love, on this basis, may be mixed up with a very different feeling, an antilove element. Ask yourself: Exactly what do I want my child to be grateful for?

Our child, who loves to be "loved," now pulls away when we try to hug and kiss him. Why doesn't he love us any more?

He loves you more than ever, and he still loves to be loved. But he is growing up, gaining steadily in independence. As he grows, he wants your love to be shown in a variety of ways. Don't discard the old ways, but add new ones, taking your lead from him. When he resists one of the old ones, just forget it.

The time comes when a child does not want Mother or Father to be hugging or kissing him at this or that particular moment. If you are having this kind of experience, why not let your child go? He has had enough "loving" for the time being. In letting him go you are respecting his wishes.

As they grow older many children, boys especially, do not want you to show affection for them in front of your guests or their own friends. It embarrasses them. It makes them feel babyish or sissy. Even such explanations as "Mother loves you" do not reconcile the growing boy to Mother's kissing him in the presence of others who are not members of the immediate family.

Again, he is not rejecting love, but only one kind of demonstration of it, in the realm of social acceptability. He does not yet understand the differences between the outside world and his home. He does know there are differences, and he is trying to determine what matters are best kept private or confidential within the family, and which can be talked about or shown in the presence of outsiders.

He is becoming a social being, and you want him to. You must help him all you can.

Our child seems to be too active. He just won't be quiet. What can we do?

In the first place, try to figure out whether he is really too active. What are your grounds for thinking so?

Is he too active for his own good?

Sometimes it does happen, of course, that a child is too active, overstimulated, when he should be ready for his nap or bedtime. On these occasions you should help him quiet down. You can do this by telling him a story, showing him pictures, reading to him.

Apart from this, it is not very likely that your child is really too active for his own good. Activity is a mechanism that automatically breeds its opposite—fatigue. The child has to give in to it before he goes too far.

The question then becomes: Is he being too active for *your* good?

Then why?

First of all, are you ill or overtired, or is there an ailing person in the home? If so, you will have to take special measures for your child's healthy, happy development. Surrounding a normally active child with restrictions, cramping the routine childish habit of yelling, jumping, tramping down the stairs, and otherwise kicking up his heels, suppresses him in ways that may reveal themselves later in life. What you *can* do depends upon your particular circumstances. A child can cooperate in a "Quiet please!" situation to a limited extent when helped to do so by your patient training, explaining, and example. The older child can, of course, do so better than the youngster. But it is sad for a child to have to grow up in a hushed sickroom atmosphere. It is hard enough on the adult, who is more in control of himself and has a better understanding of the effects of his actions on others.

If it is not illness, physical or nervous, that makes you feel your child is overactive—what is it?

Are you being fussy? Do you value the objects in your home more highly than your child's development?

Some parents do suffer from this tendency. Perhaps before the child came the mother was proud of her taste in interior decoration, of her neat-as-a-pin housekeeping.

But a growing child is often a bull in a china shop, as it were. Nothing in the world can stop even a conscientious, careful child from sometimes bumping into things, upsetting this and breaking that.

You will, of course, be training your child in the best use of objects in the home, from utensils to furniture and furnishings. You will also be teaching him to value objects, from his own clothes to the family heirlooms. But learning all this is a gradual process, requiring years.

If you own valuable objects, it is better strategy all around to put them out of the child's reach rather than depend on prohibitions. Make a special occasion of taking them down now and then, letting him examine the pretty and valuable item, telling him its story and why you prize it, showing him how lovely it is.

If among your household possessions there are expensive antiques or furnishings which must be in daily use or presence and cannot be replaced if damaged, see to it that your child's room or play space is a happy refuge for him. The child's room should be simply furnished with inexpensive, sturdy furniture, and made charming with bright-colored curtains, pillows, and bedspread. Make sure the patterns in the materials are easy to live with. The growing child can go shopping with

Mother or Daddy to pick out his own colors or designs when the washable curtains and spread wear out.

However, it is always best to have the home entirely furnished in such a way that the child can feel everything in it is his as well as yours. This is part of belonging to the family. The more forbidden territory there is, the more your child will feel excluded from your life and from your love.

Last year our daughter wanted to have music lessons, but we thought she was too young. Now she is old enough but she no longer is interested. Can you explain this?

I chose this place for the story of Margot because it brings out an aspect of time as it affects children.

Margot, at the age of seven, loved the piano. Whenever she had the opportunity she would work at the keyboard for fifteen or twenty minutes at a time, and sometimes created one-finger short melodies that were original and charming. She begged her parents to let her take lessons. They told her she must wait until she was eight years old. Their decision was based on the fact that in other families they knew, children who had begun to take instrumental lessons at six or seven seemed to have made less progress than those who began at eight. There were probably other reasons behind the decision—perhaps they started taking lessons when they were eight.

Margot tried to sit in on the piano lessons of some of her friends. She borrowed books from them and tried to learn to read music. But she could not do it by herself. Impatiently she waited for her eighth birthday. As she waited, her interest began to fade. It faded because she heard so much music inside herself and just could not bring it out on the piano. So instead of continuing to create her own music, Margot became interested in records, the radio, and television for her musical experiences.

One day her parents reminded her that soon she would be eight and could begin to take piano lessons. They were surprised when she said pleasantly and matter-of-factly, "Oh, I don't want piano lessons any more. Maybe I can have dancing lessons when I'm older."

Margot at seven could hardly wait until she was eight. But she had had to wait too long. Now the situation was reversed, for her parents waited impatiently for her to show signs of a real interest in dancing so that they could whisk her off to a dancing teacher. They realized their mistake and were not going to make the same mistake a second time.

I do not mean to tell you that if your child wants to take music lessons you should at once go and buy a piano! You know that a child has many sudden interests that are very brief, and a musical instrument is expensive. It happened that Margot's interest was real and very strong. Later, perhaps, it might be revived.

The chief point is this: For children there is usually too much "Wait until you are older." Some parents say it mechanically. Often what they really mean is "Don't bother me now," or "Don't push me," or "I'm sorry but we can't afford it." Sometimes, too, they are only saying what their own parents said to them.

Have you ever thought about the tremendous number of children all over the world who shift gears, so to speak, on a birthday? Some actually expect to feel or look different on and after *the* birthday because their parents have been saying for so long, "When you are eight (or whatever it may be). . . ."

How can a child enjoy being seven when the big things are going to happen (or so he has been given to expect) when he is eight? He lives in a kind of limbo, waiting, waiting. For children, suspense is particularly hard to endure.

No matter how much you can give and how much you can help your child, he has to endure many disappointments and has to wait for many more things than you have any idea of. Waiting often chokes off good interests and ambitions.

When you are about to say to your child, "Wait until you are older," think for a moment before you say it. Is this really the answer you want to give? Often it isn't.

Why does our child dawdle?

To understand this, you may have to look back over your child's early years.

In the beginning, when the child is learning to do things, his movements are awkward and slow. It is not hard for you to be patient because you enjoy watching him. There is such great enchantment in his fumbling, groping, examining, discovering. You are witnessing marvels. When he accomplishes his goal you enjoy it as much as he does.

But you are an adult, and you have so much to do, and suddenly the clock begins to race.

Often I have seen young children being hustled, pulled, pushed, or dragged along the street by parents who have probably found themselves late in shopping or late for an appointment. Their cause may be urgent—but not to the child, who understandably rebels by escaping from the gripping hand and scampers off, or sits down in the middle of the sidewalk, or makes himself a lead weight, or whines or cries angrily.

The harassed adult has a terrible time, just when he needs his child's cooperation.

But he has forgotten that even his leisurely pace may be faster than the child's comfortable pace. When he imposes a swift, grown-up rate upon the young child, he is working a real hardship upon him.

It will help you to remember, in this common kind of crisis, that children under five can't hurry unless they feel like it, and then only briefly. You're not likely to get good results when you say "Hurry!" to them.

Here is another experience which may be familiar to you.

You are all ready to go out, and look around for

Billy. Here he is. He has put one leg into his snowsuit and is just sitting and daydreaming as if expecting that the other leg will somehow get in by itself. This can be exasperating because you know Billy can get into his snowsuit quickly and all by himself; and besides, you are in a hurry. So you finish the job for Billy in a somewhat brusque manner. He struggles and it is a tired parent who sets out with her child on what was going to be a happy jaunt for both of them.

It is easier all around if you start getting him dressed in plenty of time and stay right there with him, not helping him but keeping him interested, until he has finished.

At this stage, dawdling does not last long if you stay with it and keep your sense of humor. If you let each incident become a crisis, the dawdling may continue indefinitely because the child begins to use it as a delaying tactic.

A parent's overconcern with getting enough of the right kinds of food into the child can start him on dawdling over his food. Serve him a small portion, with the pleasant expectation that he is going to enjoy eating it. He can always ask for a second helping.

Bedtime dawdling is a common problem, as I have discussed elsewhere. Children soon learn not to argue about going to bed if the parents themselves don't invite argument.

It is not unusual for a four- or five-year-old to say to his mother or father "Don't push me!" if he is being hurried. Nor is it uncommon for an eight- or ten-year-old to say "Give me time" when he is being accused of dawdling or of wasting time.

"Give me time!" You say it yourself sometimes when you are being hurried. It is as if time were a precious gift. And so it is, when another person has the power to give or withhold it.

The young child has to grow into the concept of time, the significance of minutes and hours. He has also to grow into the physical ability to keep pace with you and the clock.

If you have been trying to hurry your child in the early years when he is unable to hurry, he may develop a protest-habit of dawdling over any duty or at almost any time when you need his cooperation. If this is the case, although you will have to be firm where firmness is necessary, you will have to give your child more time generally for a while. This need for more time will also carry over to school, where he needs to keep up with other children.

Keep in mind that children can be helped to establish good habits when you guide them to engage only in the "quieter" activities before mealtimes and at bedtime.

When does a child learn to think and make decisions?

There is no set age. Do not discourage your child from making decisions with "You're not old enough." This is another form of "Wait until you are older," and it can retard or handicap his development.

All of us either know or work with people who find it very hard to make decisions. And we know others who spend a great deal of time vainly regretting decisions they have made. These troubles can usually be traced to early childhood, when they were forced into dependence upon others to make the decisions for them, rather than helped and encouraged to make decisions themselves.

Take the case of Mr. and Mrs. Trout and three-year-old Peter. The Trouts had moved into their new house and were struggling with the usual problems of where to place the furniture. All the rooms took shape according to their well-made plans—except Peter's. They tried several arrangements and in their absorption paid no attention to their little son. Suddenly he threw up his arms in disgust and stamped around the room shouting, "No one listens to me! It is my bed and I want it over here!"

When they tried it his way, it was fine. It had never occurred to them that a three-year-old could make a real decision—could think things out, know what he wanted, and know also that what he wanted was valid or good.

When does a child learn to think and make decisions? Recall for a moment the infant in the high chair who dropped his toy on the floor and then fussed until his mother picked it up and gave it back to him. He was thinking. In fact, infants continually engage in all kinds of experiments that require thinking.

When a child constructs a building with blocks you

can see him thinking through a series of decisions about where to put the next block in terms of balance (will the building fall over), beauty (will it look all right), function (will it serve its purpose), and so on.

Even young children know or feel which clothes they look best in, very much as you and I do. They have their favorite colors, and, like the adult, their selection of what they want to wear is in keeping with their moods. They should be encouraged to make their own selection from their wardrobe.

If the selection is wrong, don't say "No, you can't wear it because I don't want you to!" Explain why it is wrong. With your continued guidance the child learns how to dress appropriately for every occasion. Taste and discrimination are involved in the development of this everyday kind of decision-making.

Sometimes when your young daughter comes to you for approval and praise for what she has put on, you take one look and gasp. The total appearance can be rather shocking because no one item goes with any other and the color combination makes you blink. You are in a dilemma because you want to help her, but without hurting her feelings or destroying her confidence in making her own selection. It would be wise merely to suggest one small change which will make the whole outfit at least passable, instead of making her change everything.

Sometimes children will take constructive criticism more easily from others than from you. Neighbors or playmates may be brutally frank. When this happens the child's feelings may be hurt, but the hurt is temporary. The child will still accept their criticism more graciously because he is not as emotionally tied with these others as he is with you. Do not feel hurt if your child is accepting or even asking for outside criticism. He is growing into a larger kind of understanding. He is learning to take into consideration the tastes and opinions outside the home, as well as those within, in making his own decisions. He won't exclude your judgment unless you give it in a nagging manner.

The child who goes to the library is confronted with many books, but can borrow only a limited number. He is thus faced with having to make a decision which requires a lot of thinking in a short time. If he has been discouraged from making decisions, he may give the whole thing up and not go to the library again.

To make a decision, one has to be able to evaluate all the available facts, and to think clearly and sometimes also quickly. The help a child needs to develop this important ability is threefold:

1. He needs to see others in the family make decisions and be happy with them.

2. He needs to be given frequent opportunity to make his own decisions.

3. When he has made a wrong decision with unfortunate consequences, he needs sympathetic help in understanding his mistake; he should not be denied the opportunity to make more decisions just because he has made one wrong one.

Some of our child's ideas are very silly. How should we respond?

Children have many ideas. Some are excellent; others seem pretty far-fetched, but they should all be respected and listened to attentively by parents.

Here is an incident that will explain what I mean:

Mr. and Mrs. Clay were planning to buy a house and were discussing plans at the dinner table. Their daughter Florence chimed in with, "We need fifteen rooms!" Her father said, "That was a good thought, but fifteen rooms will be more than we can use." The discussion continued, and the little girl listened happily until she got tired of it. When she began to clatter her spoon on her dish, her parents changed the subject to one more interesting to her.

Florence did not know the meaning of "fifteen," and it would be some years before she would know. The word just happened to be the newest addition to her vocabulary, and she was proud to bring it out in an attempt to join in the family discussion and contribute her mite to it.

Her mother and father did not respect her idea as such. What they did respect was her right to enter the family talk, and her feeling that she should be taken seriously. And they were proud that she had managed to use her new word "fifteen" in a sensible place. Soon she was going to be having ideas worth respect in themselves.

a household chore or reading the newspaper or watching television. Your natural reaction is "Don't bother me now."

When you repeatedly rebuff a child, he is smart enough to know that there is no use in asking you questions because you don't answer them. When he asks you something, take the time from whatever you are doing and answer him. Most often it takes but a moment. Frequently a child who does not get an answer to his question searches for his own answers. These sometimes please him so much that he actually adopts as truths what he has thought out for himself. This was the case with Lois when she was four years old.

It was a cool fall evening, and Lois, surrounded by her dolls, was playing on the living room rug. Her father had lighted a fire in the fireplace and was sitting in his big chair reading the evening paper. Several times Lois had interrupted his reading with questions and he had answered her. Finally he asked that she wait until he had finished the newspaper.

Lois went on playing, but every time she looked up her father was still reading. Her mother came into the room, gave Lois a loving pat on the head, threw a few pieces of torn paper into the fireplace, and left the room. Lois watched the paper burn, become a thin sheet of ash, and disappear up the chimney.

"Daddy, where did that burned paper go?" Lois asked excitedly. She could hardly wait for the answer to this amazing thing she had seen. But her father was still absorbed in his reading. Lois sat there puzzled for a moment, and then turned to her dolls. Here is the story she told them:

"You saw Mother throw that paper in the fire, didn't you? When she threw it in, the paper was thick newspaper. When it burned it got thin and gray. It was so thin that when the wind blew, the paper went up the chimney, and it kept right on going up and up in the sky, until it got to the place where the angels live. The angels save it and use it for their toilet tissue. Mother put it in the fire to burn and blow away because she knew the angels needed it."

Lois had worked it all out, and it was no longer a mystery to her. I was sitting on the sofa, knitting, and I enjoyed her story and her happy satisfaction with it. This happened many years ago, and Lois is now the mother of four young children. Their home has a fireplace, and I wonder if any of her children has also been curious about the ash paper that goes up the chimney. What would her answer be? Maybe she still prefers to believe what she told her dolls so many years ago.

The incident was charming and did no harm. But it might have. If Lois had not been so happy with her own answer, she might have been led to experiment with matches and paper, in much the spirit of the scientist who is trying to find out why and how something happens. The scientist takes the necessary safety precautions. The child doesn't know how to do so. Daddy's absorption in his newspaper might well have had grave consequences.

A child expresses his thoughts in various ways, and sometimes you can't make out what he is thinking. When you listen carefully, you can usually tell whether he is searching for clarification of his ideas, asking you for help, or wanting you to understand how he feels about things. His trust in you is so great that when it is shaken, it is as if one of the props of the world has crumbled.

One day, waiting to board a plane, I witnessed an exchange between a father and his son, who appeared to be about six years old.

"What are you looking at, Daddy?" the boy asked.

"A magazine I bought at the newsstand," his father replied shortly, not glancing at his son.

The boy hesitated, looked down, and made a few movements with his right foot on the cement floor. Then he asked, "Daddy, why didn't you buy me the comic book when you bought the magazine? I asked you to."

"I forgot," the father said, still immersed in his magazine.

The boy's face had a puzzled expression, and he seemed unsure how to continue. He waited for almost a full minute. He looked around at the people who were standing in line, and at those who walked by toward another gate.

At last he looked up at his father, and with great courage asked, "Why did you forget to buy my comic book, Daddy?"

His father closed his magazine abruptly, frowned at his son, and said, "I didn't forget. I didn't buy it because I don't want you to have any more comic books.

You have too many already. Now, does that answer your question?"

I shall never forget the small boy's look of hurt. He was hurt deeply, not only because he didn't get the comic book, but—what was more serious—because his father had lied to him. He was shaken, and even more unsure of himself, but his courage was admirable. With a choked voice he asked, "Why did you say you forgot when you didn't really forget?"

At this moment the announcement came over the loudspeaker that the plane was ready for boarding. The line began to move. I shall never know what the father answered to the boy's brave question, or if he answered at all.

Why did this father tell his son that he forgot to buy the comic book if that was not the truth? Perhaps he felt that this answer would satisfy his son and cut off further discussion. But if he didn't want his son to have a comic book he should have said so right off and explained his reasons.

It will take time and wise judgment and behavior for this father to win back his son's confidence. Think of the predicament he'll be in if, hereafter, he tries to discipline his son for telling a falsehood!

Some children are not satisfied with a "No, you can't have it," even when an explanation accompanies it. Some will keep on asking, nagging and whining, until you feel so harassed that you lose your temper. The child who is always given an explanation along with the firm "No" does less of this sort of thing.

If your child keeps on asking for the comic book, or whatever else it is that he wants so much, does this mean that you should buy it for him?

Not if you are convinced that he should not have it. But he is always entitled to an honest answer.

I want our child to play but my husband says he should help out more around the house. Which of us is right?

The child needs a mixed diet of work and play. The work should not be too much for him, however; nor should it be sternly imposed. His desires, interests, and abilities should be taken into account.

The spirit should be one of cooperation. Wholehearted cooperation is the greatest strength any family group can have. It gives to each individual a fine feeling of pride both in himself and in his family.

In every family, the mother and father have their work. The child wants to work too. He wants his share in this important aspect of life in order to feel that he is a part of the family. When he's restricted to all play and no work, he feels excluded from the family as a unit, a team.

Four-year-old Carol asked her father one evening, "Why does Mother have to work so hard?" Her father was startled. Could such a young child be aware of all that her mother did to make everyone happy? He wisely decided to let Carol express herself more fully. The little girl explained that she had offered to help her mother wash the kitchen floor, and later to run the vacuum cleaner. Each time her mother told her to go and play, that she would do it herself.

It was then that Carol's father realized that his daughter had a grievance. She felt hurt.

He talked it over with his wife. Up to now Carol had been permitted to help her mother set the table and to wipe a few dishes. Her mother appreciated her offers to help, but was refusing them because she thought she was being kind in doing so. She wanted her daughter to have an entirely happy childhood. She now saw her error; her idea of happiness was not her daughter's. She understood that for Carol the few things she had been permitted to help with were easy little chores. Carol knew she could do more, and wanted to. She was hurt because she felt excluded from helping with the really important jobs.

And there was eight-year-old Mike, who rang the doorbell of a neighbor, Mrs. Ward, and asked if he could rake her leaves. "Don't you think," he said, "that it would be a nice surprise for Mr. Ward when he comes home?" Mrs. Ward thought it a splendid idea and asked Mike how much he would charge. "Oh, it won't cost you anything, Mrs. Ward. I'll do it because you're too busy," Mike answered.

Mike went to work and did a thorough job. When he finished, he went home. Mrs. Ward, discovering he had gone, phoned to thank him. "Oh, that's O.K.," he said. "I liked it." Mrs. Ward couldn't get over this. "What a wonderful boy!" she kept saying.

Mike *was* a wonderful boy, but he was not just being neighborly. A few days before, while Mike was at school, his busy and hard-working mother raked the leaves from their own lawn to give Daddy a nice surprise. It had not occurred to her to let her son in on the surprise for Daddy, and to let him rake the leaves, giving him the pleasure and responsibility that he would have loved. Mike was so deeply hurt at having been excluded that he tried to ease his hurt in a very good way—by acting out the son's role for Mr. and Mrs. Ward. But it was not the same thing, of course. The hurt remained.

And Alice.

Alice and her mother decided the kitchen floor needed scrubbing. Alice took her small pail, and her mother the large one. "You start at that end and I will start over here," Alice directed.

They went to work and there was little conversation because it was a hard job and they were both very busy. When they finished, they stood in the kitchen doorway and admired their work. "Oh, look!" Alice cried, pointing. Sure enough, there was a place along the cupboard that her mother had missed. Quickly Alice ran over and took care of that place. Then, joining her mother again, she said, "Don't worry, Mother. We all make mistakes. It happens to me sometimes."

Whether Alice was using the consoling technique

that her mother used with her in the past, or whether she was being humorous over her mother's error, doesn't matter in the least. The rapport between Alice and her mother was beautiful.

Children really want to share in the family work as well as in the family fun. It gives them the feeling of being needed.

By the way, they recognize very quickly whether the job is a real one, or just something that you dreamed up to keep them busy. And they dislike the made-up job. Don't we all?

When should we give our child an allowance?

This depends on the child's interest in money and his need for an allowance. Some children are ready for an allowance at the age of five. Others show no interest until six or seven.

A child usually wants an allowance when his friends are getting one. He sees their pride in having money, and sees them buying what they want; while he himself has to run to his mother or father to ask for money, and often is not permitted to handle it himself but only watch while his parent buys the small item he wants.

Whatever your child's age, before you begin to give him a regular weekly allowance you should first discuss with him the use of money. This discussion should not be a set lecture. It can take place over a period of time.

For example, it might begin when, parking the car beside a meter, you give your youngster the coin to put into the slot, or when you let your child pay for a newspaper. Sometimes he gets change, which creates many questions for you to answer.

Find opportunities to let your child handle money under your supervision so that he can learn its uses and its value. If you do this, he will be ready for an allowance by the time he asks for one.

Since each member of the family uses money, the child is soon going to want to use it too. Behind many a child's desire for money is the determination to save it in order to buy Mother or Daddy a present. It may be many weeks before he actually does succeed in carrying out his purpose, but when he does it is a great achievement and he feels great joy for having done it. For now he can buy something for others, just as they buy for him. The desire to save money is often very strong in a child. Or the exact opposite may be true. Should your child want to spend his money too quickly he needs more casual but effective help in learning to hold on to it until he sees what he really wants.

Our ten-year-old spends money foolishly. How can we help to give him a sense of values?

You cannot "give" anyone a sense of values. It has to be learned. It is learned through many experiences. Foremost among them is the good example set by the parents in what they buy, and in their evaluation or judgment of its worth in terms of cost, quality, usefulness, or beauty.

Many children get an early lesson in values when making a trade. Often one of the traders gets hurt or cheated by giving up something of real value for something worth very little. This is a hard lesson for the child to learn, but it is usually a good one, and his parents should let him experience the consequences of his own decisions and judgment. This would not be wise, of course, if it were a case of a much older child taking advantage of a young child or if it is a young child who has lost something of too great value.

In the second case, the object of "real" value—by which I mean costly—may have been of comparatively small value to the child himself. He may not have cared for it much. So you would have to explain how and why it is of much greater value than what he traded it for.

Values are relative.

The child who spends all his weekly allowance in one day or two days discovers the value of his allowance and begins to test it against the store or price value of what he wants, and also the value (much more difficult to assess) of these things to himself.

Suppose he wants certain comic books and a bag of marbles, but hasn't the money for both. If the other children in the neighborhood are playing marbles, he may decide that the marbles are more valuable to him because he wants to get into the games. So, although he wants the comic books very much, he will give them up as having less value, for now.

He may, however, decide for the marbles because he can trade his old comic books with his friends for others he hasn't read; or because he can persuade his parents to buy him the books. In either case he is displaying good judgment and a sense of values on a very practical level.

You and your child together should decide what is the best day for him to receive his allowance. Some children who receive it on Saturday are inclined to spend all of it that day because there is no school and they can go shopping. Others who receive it on Monday find it somewhat easier to make it last the whole week.

When you give your child an allowance, make it clear both to him and to yourselves how much it is expected to cover. If comic books can be had only through the allowance, the child will keep this in mind when he is spending his money. But if they are not, or if he knows that even though they are he can persuade Mother or Daddy to give way on this point, he will keep that in mind too when he spends.

How can we teach our child about credit?

Credit is a word and concept used in several different ways.

One form has to do with honesty and fair play, giving the other fellow the credit for his idea. The child learns this in his family when he is given the credit for something he has thought up, and is corrected when he claims credit for another's idea. The correction should be without blame. Among his playmates and at school, he is also corrected in this way.

Another form is expressed in "your credit is good." Here your reputation is really meant.

My father taught me a lesson when I was eleven years old, one I have cherished ever since. He held up to the light a plate of fine china so that I could see the shadow of his fingers through it. He said, slowly and carefully, "Your credit is like this beautiful piece of china. It is very fragile. If you break it, it can be mended—but it will never be the same."

My father had carefully laid the foundation before he taught me this valuable lesson. He had been building toward it for years, and not until he saw I was ready did he give me this practical illustration with which to complete my understanding. Knowing your child as you do, find the right time and the best illustration for him.

Money-credit is still another thing, although it is closely allied with reputation-credit.

Why you can walk out of a store with a package under your arm, without giving the clerk any money, is a mystery to children. It can be explained: "I can buy this now without paying because the man knows he can trust me to pay later. He will send me a bill at the end of the month and I will pay him then for everything I

bought this way all that month. I can only do this because my credit is good."

At home you can show him the bills as they come
in, and show him also how you pay by check.

The child is bound to have difficulty understanding
just what this credit is. The huge concept of living
within one's means must be part of this learning experience.

All of us know people who buy more than they can
pay for because it is so convenient to use charge accounts or delayed-paying plans such as "a dollar down
and a dollar a week." In the credit plan of "buy now,
pay later," the "later" is for some adults much the same
as "later" is to the child—far away, and never-never.

When parents live within their means, the child can
more easily learn that credit is not a special kind of game
played by grownups; it is a responsibility.

I shall never forget eight-year-old Ruth's concern
when her father asked her for the loan of a quarter from
her piggy-bank because he had no change for busfare
in the morning. "When will you pay it back?" she asked.
"Tomorrow," said her father.

Ruth could hardly wait for Daddy to come home
the next evening. He hadn't even taken off his coat
when she was asking for her quarter. He gave her the
quarter and thanked her for extending him credit for
twenty-four hours. She was a very proud and happy
little girl, and she had learned a great deal about money
and credit.

How soon should we let our son have a bank account?

Some children have a bank account and don't know anything about it. The account has been opened and is being kept up by the parents, or by relatives, for his future, usually for college. The youngster is told that he has money in the bank but cannot touch it until (and a time is named which for him is so far ahead that he really cannot visualize it). The money in the bank then means nothing to him. Rather, it is a puzzle—he has money but he cannot use it; so has he really got money, or not? He feels vaguely important, but the whole thing doesn't make much sense to him.

It can begin to make some sense to him if he is taken by his mother or father to the bank when they are depositing or withdrawing from their own accounts. He can then see what a bank is, and how one uses it.

The best time, of course, for your child to have a bank account of his own—one that he can use—is when he is earning money of his own.

Should we let our child take a job?

Surely you will let him take a job if he is ready to assume such a responsibility.

When your child goes to work at his first job for

money, he is taking a big step out into the world. He needs your approval, and in giving it wholeheartedly you are taking the big step with him.

He may get his first job as early as six or seven years old, raking leaves for a neighbor; at ten or twelve he may be delivering newspapers; in the early teens, baby sitting. Whatever the job is, something new and different and grown up has come into his life. He is working for pay, and this pay is to him real money in a way that no other can be.

Many children decide how they are going to spend this money long before they have earned it. Some even go window-shopping to look over items and their prices; and on the great day—payday—they count the money, hold on to it very carefully, and are off like a shot to spend it. Others wait until the money is in their possession before they begin to think about what to do with it.

Whether your child does this thinking before or after he is paid, your role in helping him to decide what to do with it is of great importance. It is a role of guidance, but without any pressure on your part. You listen to his ideas, discuss them with him, and suggest alternatives that he may not have considered. But the decision itself should be his.

You may wish to teach him to bank a part of everything he earns, now and later. He will want to know, quite naturally, what he is saving it for. Because the future is far away and dim—particularly to children under eight—you will have to be very realistic in your explanation.

In talking with him about his money, you will also be trying to help him to evaluate his desires, so that he becomes more clearly aware of the fact that there are things of lasting value to him, as against those that are used up right away.

He may have the burning desire to buy something that his friends have. If so, in encouraging or discouraging him, bear in mind that adults do this kind of buying too—"keeping up with the Joneses," we call it.

If he decides what he wants to do and you say "You can't buy that because it is a foolish way to spend your money," you are not giving him the opportunity to evaluate his own thinking, understand all the alternatives you may suggest, and finally make the decision. So he doesn't learn much from the entire experience except, perhaps, resentment. He will feel "You're not fair," or "You always make me do what you want, and I don't have a chance."

What he decides may turn out to be against your better judgment. But if he has made a poor decision, he will find it out for himself. After all, it is *his* money.

We want our child to develop an interest in a fine career. How can we help him do this?

Your child's life is his own, not yours. Sometimes this is hard to remember. Do you really want to "make" him become something he doesn't want to be, or keep him from what he does want to be? This may seem a harsh question.

I am taking up this question because many parents have strong feelings, from the very beginning, about what career they want their child to follow, and encourage or discourage him accordingly.

Annette, Mrs. Wise's daughter, at the early age of seven, had decided that she wanted to be a nurse when she grew up. No one knew where she had got this idea, but there was no question of her strong interest and serious determination. Her mother was firmly against it. She had a great respect for the nursing profession, but felt that it was not for her Annette.

One afternoon, Annette did not come home from school. After an hour Mrs. Wise, in great alarm, set out to look for her. She couldn't find her anywhere, so she hurried home to call her husband. The phone was ringing, however, when she returned. It was the family doctor. Annette, he said, was with him. She had walked more than two miles from her school to his office. Her first words were: "Dr. Beck, I have come to be your office nurse. I have practiced everything on my dolls. Now I am ready to work with you on real people."

The little girl, when handed the phone, said, "Don't be angry with me, Mother. I want to be a nurse so I can take care of you when you get sick."

Mrs. Wise decided to say nothing further about Annette's choice of a career. In another year, the little girl's interest in nursing seemed to be forgotten.

When Annette entered high school, she began to have serious talks with her parents about the positions and professions open to women. One evening, when they were discussing the subject, her mother suggested that she consider studying to become a nurse. "You would make such a good one!" she remarked.

Annette looked up and said, "I don't want to be a nurse. You killed that idea when I was little, don't you remember?"

When Jonathan Williams was five, his mother decided that he must be a surgeon when he grew up. She bought toys which she thought would teach him to use his fingers with dexterity. She filled his library with books about medicine and surgery. She would not let him participate in active games for fear that he might suffer a hand injury. All through his early and later childhood she tried in every way to make him feel dedicated to the great career she had chosen for him, and did not permit him to discuss any other.

In his junior year in college, Jonathan told his mother that he intended to be an engineer. She couldn't believe it. She felt that he was being terribly cruel to her. But in return he reminded her of all that she had deprived him of during his childhood, which hurt her a great deal. The cleavage between mother and son was tragic, and very nearly permanent. There was much pain and emotional suffering for both of them. But Jonathan did become an engineer, and his mother is proud of him.

Many fathers look forward to the day when their

sons will take over their business or enter their profession. These fathers should bear in mind that their own chosen work may not interest their sons.

The boy who does not want to join his father in the business is not showing ingratitude. He may know that he is not fit for this kind of work, or he may want to try other things before he decides what he wants to do with his life.

From the beginning, encourage your child to choose for himself what he wants to become. Why else do you help him to learn to think for himself? It should be with great parental pride and pleasure that you help your child grow in all directions so that he can gather his forces—all that you have wisely and lovingly taught him—to make, carefully and thoughtfully, one of the greatest decisions of his life.

✳⥽☙⥼✳⥽☙⥼✳⥽☙⥼✳⥽☙⥼✳⥽☙

Our child becomes a social being

✳⥽☙⥼✳⥽☙⥼✳⥽☙⥼✳⥽☙⥼✳⥽☙

Is it important for our child to have friends his own age?

Yes, it is. Your child need others of his approximate age and size to play with day after day. Occasionally he can have fun with older or younger children. But even the best-behaved eight- or ten-year-old cannot help pushing a four- or six-year-old around at times. Young children can also be very annoying to those who are older because they tag along, ask too many questions, and get in the way.

If there are no children in your community of your own child's approximate age, try to arrange to have children in from other neighborhoods, and also have him visit them. This should be regularly scheduled. Early attendance at a good nursery school is very helpful, and makes such arrangements easier.

Soon after a child's second birthday he becomes genuinely interested in other children. Until then, he likes to have them around, whatever their age, even though there may be conflicts (by these small battles he begins to learn of their rights or demands as against his own).

After the age of two, he feels a certain kinship with them—he is reaching out socially. However, he is still too young to join in group play. More often, you see him quietly playing with his toys beside the other children, and although he likes their nearness he sometimes resents it if they intrude upon what he is doing.

At three, the child is a social being, joining in many activities with others. He is now having important personal experiences in conflict and cooperation, in the exchange of ideas, and in leadership and "follow-the-leadership." From now on he grows steadily in social relationships with other children.

When a child has had little or no opportunity to grow with other children of his approximate age, he may have serious social difficulties when he begins school, and even later. Learning to get along with other children when he is in kindergarten or first grade often interferes with his learning to read or work on group projects.

Should we let our child bring his friends to our house every day? It makes so much extra work.

It isn't necessary for him to bring his friends home every day, although the fact that he does, or wants to do so, shows that he feels the need to do it. It shows something more—that you have created a warm and friendly atmosphere in your home which your child loves, and which his friends love too.

The visiting, however, can be restricted to several times a week. When you explain the restriction, ask for your child's cooperation and give him some of the responsibility for the extra work. You can have a few rules, such as using the back door instead of the front, if this is important to you.

Parents should encourage their child, from an early age, to bring his friends home.

You want to know his friends, and to see how he is getting along with them. When they play in your home, you have the best opportunity to look into your child's broadening personal world, distinct from the one he shares entirely with you.

By this encouragement you are also building for the future; you will want to meet his grade school, high school, and college friends. When you keep the door closed to his friends, you cannot know what kind of friends he is making; and if one or another of them is leading him into doing something wrong, he is not likely to come to you for advice and guidance.

From the beginning, your warm interest and observation is important for your child's developing sociability, and over a period of time his behavior with his playmates can be revealing to you. In many ways you may see where he needs your help. He may be too easily intimidated by others, or too aggressive, withdrawn, or dominated.

When your child is with his playmates, watch him now and then—keeping yourself well in the background —and check on these points:

1. How well does he communicate his ideas to them?

2. Do they understand him easily, or does he have to repeat many times?

3. Are his ideas accepted, ignored or laughed at, and are they for the most part good ideas?

4. Does he hold his head up and look at the others when talking, or does he look at the floor?

5. Is he often interrupted, or does he himself interrupt most of the time?

6. Does he talk only when another child asks him a question? Or does he find it difficult to stop talking and give the others their turn?

7. Have the other children given him a nickname which they use as a label, such as "Slow poke" or "Bashful"?

Our daughter has good manners but behaved badly at a party. Does this mean that she is antisocial or that I have not prepared her properly for such an experience?

No. It only means that for some reason she did not behave well upon one occasion. You may not be able to find out why immediately, but you can talk it over with her. Do not make her feel that she has done something so disgraceful that she is a social outcast.

Mrs. Franklin's well-mannered daughter Rita was invited to Marcia's birthday party. Rita looked forward to the affair, and when the day and time came she left looking lovely and happy in her new dress, and carefully carrying a beautifully wrapped gift for her friend.

The party was a success until the children were called to the table. Rita discovered that Marcia's mother was serving a gelatin dessert with the birthday cake. She refused to go to the table. When asked what the trouble was, she screamed: "I don't like that! I can't eat it! I'm going home!" Marcia's mother finally persuaded her to join the others by promising to serve her sliced peaches.

When Rita came home, her mother asked her about the party. She described it in such a way that her mother was pleased and said, "What a nice party!"

Several days later, Marcia came to Rita's home to

play with her. She told Mrs. Franklin about her nice party, and what she said was like Rita's report, with one exception—she told of the dessert incident. She added, "Mother said Rita was not a very nice girl at my party."

Mrs. Franklin was quite shocked. Rita busied herself with her toys and said nothing.

After Marcia had gone home, Mrs. Franklin discussed the birthday party again with Rita. She did not scold. She did not lecture. She did not even ask Rita why she had behaved so badly. There was a quiet, serious, heart-to-heart talk about what one does as a guest in someone's home—about the pleasant role and obligations of host or hostess, and of guest.

At the end, Rita said, "Please don't tell Daddy when he gets home!"

Mrs. Franklin assured her that she would not tell Daddy, or anyone else. The incident was over and done with.

This mother understood that her daughter had told her a "lie of omission" because she was ashamed of herself and a little bit afraid to tell her mother. Rita knew that she had behaved badly, and it had been weighing on her conscience. Now that her mother knew all, Rita felt that she had to have an end to this painful experience.

She was right, and her mother knew this too.

Parents, and teachers too, sometimes keep reminding children of their past errors or blunders. Their intention is good, but mistaken.

Many lessons in getting along with people, and of considerate and courteous behavior—social lessons—are painfully learned. No one needs to be reminded of such experiences, for they leave a deep impression. When adults do this sort of thing, they not only call up pain and shame, but make the child feel he will never be permitted to live it down. In one way or another he rejects this burden.

By the way, tattling, although of course resented, is not always a serious offense among children. Marcia was hurt by Rita's behavior at her party, and felt righteous—the tattler usually does! Rita was hurt by Marcia's tattling. But each forgave the other, and they remained friends.

How can we teach our child to behave well when we visit friends who have no children he can play with?

Such visits should be brief. A child cannot sit very long and listen politely to adult conversation which has nothing to do with him.

Sometimes when adults get together, those who are close friends become absorbed in exchanging news or talking of mutual and special interests, and forget about a newcomer introduced by one of them. Have you, as a new acquaintance, ever had this kind of experience?

There you sit, fidgeting, wishing with all your heart you had never come, while conversation swirls about you. Such discomfort sometimes becomes acute.

A child feels much the same on a visit to adults who are not really interested in him.

When you take your child even on a brief visit to someone you think loves children, it is wise to make certain in advance that this person really does love and understand children and plans something for him to do when he comes.

Christopher's mother took him to visit a friend of his grandmother's, an elderly woman who loved children and particularly wanted to see Chris, whom she had not seen since he was a baby four years ago. Chris and his mother got all dressed up for the visit. It was a cool autumn day and Christopher wore his new jacket and cap. He was especially proud of the cap because it had a visor.

Miss Maple, their hostess, greeted them at the door and was happy to see them. She exclaimed over how Chris had grown, and what a nice big boy he was. But when she asked to take their wraps, Chris would not remove his new cap. She insisted. Chris looked at the floor and hung on to his precious cap. Miss Maple then launched into a lecture on the rudeness of boys who wear their hats indoors, and especially in the presence of women. The lecture was intended for Christopher's young mother who was thus told that she was not bringing up her son properly.

The two visitors did not stay long. On their way home, Christopher's mother explained Miss Maple's behavior merely by saying that Miss Maple did not understand certain things about small boys. But she added that it really was a rule of good behavior for a boy to remove his hat or cap, just as Miss Maple had said, and that she hoped Chris would do this in the future.

Our daughter loves to visit her grandmother, but on her return keeps asking whether we missed her. Doesn't she know that we missed her?

Everyone wants to feel that he is missed when he is away. In children the need is even stronger than in grownups because they do not take your love for granted.

When a child asks "Did you miss me?" the look of hope on his face is touching. When you say "Yes, we missed you so much!" joy and love permeate his body. But if the answer indicates in any way that you didn't miss him, he droops. The disappointment goes deep and is not forgotten. He may be less willing to leave the next time.

The child's first day in nursery school or kindergarten may bring the same question, and also the first few times he is away from you briefly, for lunch or dinner with friends or relatives.

He may not ask at all. If he doesn't, the question is certain to be inside him anyway. You see it in the swift rush of his entrance, and then the stopping and looking around. In the next minute or so, what you say or fail to say will bring him happiness or grief.

Don't wait for him to ask you if you missed him. Tell him so. Show him how happy you and everyone in the family are to have him back. Tell him what has been going on while he was gone.

You should also ask him about what he did away from you. But if you ask a question like "What did you do at Grandmother's?" he is likely to answer "Nothing." It is for him an overwhelming question; he did so many things! If you ask something specific like "What did Grandmother make for your breakfast this morning?" you give him a starting point from which he can go on.

Do not expect or insist upon a full report. Let him tell as much as he wants to. Often, a day or two later, he will be coming up with something else that happened during the time he was away having experiences without you. Or it may be a couple of weeks later, when you serve beans for dinner, that he will tell you how Grandmother fixed them.

Our child is away at camp and doesn't write to us. How can we encourage him to do this?

When children go off to camp, or on an extended vacation, the situation is usually reversed—that is, the parents become fully, and even painfully, aware that they miss him and want to know that he misses them. The first time is often very hard on the parents. When mothers and fathers are seeing their young children off to camp, you can observe many of them struggling bravely with their emotions.

It is at this time of separation that letter-writing becomes important.

The best way to begin is—simply to begin! I mean just that. Begin by writing to your child, telling him that you miss him, asking him if he is getting a chance to enjoy his favorite activities, and put other simple questions that he can answer easily. Give a little of the home news, and end by saying you want him to write back because it means so much to you to hear from him.

I know a mother and father who began practice in correspondence with their child before he left on his vacation. They explained it to him first, but it didn't mean very much to him. They then wrote him a letter, mailed it, and he received it and read it all by himself. It was then that letter-writing became exciting to him, for he at once wrote them a funny note, and mailed it; he could hardly wait for the mailman to bring it, and stood by watching while they opened and read it.

I repeat that the best way to begin is—to begin. If you think about what a "correct" letter should be, how it should look, and try to form literary words and sentences, you'll find yourself staring at blank paper.

Your child, when he is away, is having something of the same problem. Even when children have had instruction in letter-writing, both at home and at school, writing to their parents is a new and rather strange experience. They are so much a part of him; he cannot really conceive of them as being not here. Some of the first letters of parents to children and of children to parents should be treasured, not alone for themselves but for all that is behind them.

Eight-year-old George Spaulding was asked by his camp counselor one day why he had not written home. He said, "My mother knows everything I do. She knows I'm having a good time now."

The counselor explained that she had no way of knowing, and it took a lot of explaining before George understood. When he did, he sat down and carefully wrote his letter. His mother, when she opened it, read: "Dear Mrs. Spaulding. . . ." Her shock was great. How could her warm, outgoing son, with whom she had such a happy understanding, address her in this formal manner? Her anxiety caused her to write to the counselor.

George explained to him in this way: "I respect my mother, and I wrote so that when the mailman read my letter he would know I said it the right way. Anyhow, this is the way all letters are written."

To George, a letter was not a private affair. It had a long way to travel, and he wanted his letter to be correct so that the postman, who was in his mind the Guardian Angel of the Mails, would approve of it and would know that George Spaulding respected his mother.

Another camp counselor told me about Dick, who like George was having his first camp experience. The first letter he received from home was from his father, and it began, "Dear Son. . . ."

Dick had never been called "Son" by his father or mother, and he was just as concerned about this as Mrs. Spaulding was when she received George's letter. Dick had many long talks with the counselor. He wanted to know why things were different now. Was this what camp was supposed to do? Was everything going to be changed when he got home? Was he going to be "Son" from now on?

Not until his father visited him was he reassured.

The contents of these first letters are sometimes worrying. The child approaches the letter with great anticipation, and he cannot read between the lines, as an adult can. He reads only what is written.

It is not always easy for you to write a happy letter to your child. You may be very unhappy indeed, missing him. Nor is it a simple task to tell him how much you miss him without making him homesick or troubled because he is having a good time while you are so sad.

Take time to read your letter after you have written it, to make sure it has the right tone.

Our nine-year-old daughter loves to receive gifts but hates to write thank-you notes. What do you suggest?

Many adults find letter-writing very difficult too, even when only a short note is required. That is probably why there are so many cards in the shops covering so many situations, from "Thank you" to "Sorry you're ill," to which you have only to sign your name.

But a handwritten note is more intimate. What is more, your child can become aware of his social obligations when he is encouraged to get into the habit of writing.

It is a good habit. Both the writer and the receiver of the note or letter have pleasure and satisfaction. Many friends, and even close relatives, are lost to one another when separated for a time simply because they do not write.

To return to the question itself: Your daughter may not be writing her thank-you notes because she doesn't know what to put down on the paper.

Help her by giving her three or four different ways of expressing her appreciation for the gift, and let her select the one she likes best. The next time, you can say, "Just tell Aunt Mary you like her gift very much—in your own words, just as if you were talking to her." And if she again "blanks out," sit beside her and help her patiently until she has written the note. Praise her by saying, "I think Aunt Mary is going to be pleased."

If your daughter has written notes in the past so that you know she can do it but hates the task, insist that she do it. You want her to understand that consideration for others is behind even the simplest courtesy. Explaining this, make an assignment of the writing of the note, to be completed by a certain time. See that she has completed her assignment in the given time.

*Our child doesn't seem to like people, not
even other children, and prefers to be alone.
Is this abnormal?*

First look for the reason. Perhaps he has been hurt by
someone, or has seen others hurt by an unfortunate experience. Help him to understand and accept what has
happened, rather than let him withdraw into himself.

One who withdraws is putting up a wall between
himself and others, usually for a sense of safety. This is
the wrong kind of self-protection because generally there
is no happiness in loneliness. You want your child not
only to learn how to get along with people, but to enjoy
being with them.

Usually, a child reflects his parents' feeling for
people. If you enjoy friends in for lunch, dinner, or the
evening, and along on walks or drives, your child generally accepts this sociability as a natural and joyful part of
family living. Children will show their affection for their
friends in much the same way. They will enjoy them.

*Our son is quiet and well-mannered at home,
but is the opposite when he visits his friends.
Can you explain this? Is he two different
persons?*

In a way, he is two different persons; and it is much
better for him, of course, to be one person.

There are children who have been in some way overpowered by their parents, and because they have to repress themselves so much in the home, they become very aggressive outside. There are others who do exactly the opposite. They are usually shy, and if they are dominated by aggressive children for a long time they may have frequent emotional outbursts at home.

These are troubled children, but they have spirit. They can stand being overpowered for only so long— and then have to explode.

They should be encouraged in every possible way to gain the self-confidence which will help combat the aggressions of others. Sometimes parents cannot do this themselves and will require outside professional help.

My young daughter is demanding a permanent and I refuse to let her have one. Should I give in?

Nowadays some mothers begin to take their daughters to the beauty salon when the little ones are scarcely more than tots. I have seen over the years the results of this kind of practice. Some of the girls not only have permanents but they have manicures also; or else Mother herself applies the nail polish. Often the child tries to take care of the hairdo and her nails as Mother wants her to, and is torn between her need for healthy, happy play and the desire to look like her mother's idea of a glamour girl. Giving children permanents and manicures when they are still little girls tends toward robbing them of their childhood.

If your daughter is clamoring for a permanent, it is probably because other girls in the neighborhood have them. To her innocent eyes it appears grown-up, and she wants to be like her friends.

It is in such situations—where social pressure and social prestige seem to be involved—that you must think about what is best for your child.

Tell your daughter that you love her as she is and do not want to make her over into another kind of person. You may then encourage her yearning to be feminine by concentrating on personal hygiene. A pretty bottle of scented bath salts all for herself, and a comb-and-brush set with her initials can work wonders.

You must also be interested in her clothes, and give her greater freedom of choice in what she wants to wear. There should be mother-and-daughter talks about fashions, and in shopping let her try on things different from those she has been wearing. Decide together what looks the most becoming for her individuality. You might also suggest or let her try a new-style haircut.

Be very careful not to criticize the other girls and their mothers. You are not concerned with them, but only with your own daughter's desire to be attractive. It is a natural desire. The fact that it begins to blossom earlier in the young generation than it did in ours does not make it "unnatural." It only means that your daughter is responding to a social development of which we had no experience in our own childhood because it did not exist then.

When you see this, you realize that a stern *No!* does not meet the situation, but only raises a barrier between the child and her parents. On the other hand, the indulgent *Yes* does not teach anything; it only encourages your daughter to do what others are doing for no other reason than that they are doing it. By interest, sessions before the mirror, heart-to-heart talks, you can help your daughter develop a constructive pride in herself as an individual.

Our son, ten, wants to go steady with a little girl-friend of nine. Don't you think this is ridiculous?

I know how you feel, and it does seem ridiculous from an adult point of view. But in many communities early dating among children has become a social custom. This is something new, and I have no idea how or where it began.

Among these children, "going steady" really doesn't mean much. There may be an exchange of pins or bracelets, and the boy will be visiting a little more often, and perhaps once or twice he will want to escort the girl to a friend's birthday party.

If your son wants to "go steady" you will find that

others of his age are doing this. Since what is involved differs from one neighborhood or community to another, it would be wise to consult the parents of the girl, and also other neighbors whose children are having fun in this way, to learn the local rules of the practice. Such customs always have quite definite rules.

Of course you will also ask your son to explain it to you, in order to know what he understands by "going steady."

When all of you know what this is all about, then you and your son and the girl and her parents can have a mutual understanding of what may take place. This will include the freedoms as well as the limitations the children are to have.

Our eight-year-old often annoys our guests by insisting that they play with him. How can we break him of this habit?

Often a child feels excluded from activities when guests are present. When this happens something seems to drive him to get the grownups to entertain him and thus make him happy.

Some practical measures can be taken for this specific problem.

1. Talk with your child before the guests arrive, explaining that Mother and Daddy have a lot of things

to talk about with the guests which may not interest him. He may listen as long as he cares to, but he may not make demands.

2. Plan together some special project he will enjoy working on alone after dinner. It may be one of those do-it-yourself kits, like making a model airplane or boat; or he may engage in some research for a new experiment he wants to try; or read a book.

3. Let him invite a guest of his own, a friend, to work on some quiet, absorbing project with him, and perhaps stay overnight.

✽⤙✿⤙✽⤙✿⤙✽⤙✿⤙✽⤙✿⤙✽⤙✿

School bells

✽⤙✿⤙✽⤙✿⤙✽⤙✿⤙✽⤙✿⤙✽⤙✿

Our son, who must start school next month, insists he won't go. Why should he feel this way?

He should be looking forward to it. Since he is not, it means that he is worried and afraid. Help him to feel happy about going. Tell him that he will like school very much, that it will be great fun for him. If you believe this, he will feel it and be less troubled.

The child prepares for school long before he is of school age. When he is a toddler just learning about things in the world, he learns the words *school, teacher, playground, class.* As he grows he absorbs more and more about school, teacher, playground, class, and the like; he connects them as having to do with children and with himself.

He learns about school from you, from the books you are reading to him, from the stories you tell him. He learns also from other children, some of whom begin school before he himself is of age; he sees older children going. Relatives, your friends, and even casual acquaintances make remarks to him such as, "You're growing so fast that before we know it you'll be in school."

As the day nears when the bell will ring for him, he has already been saying and thinking for a long time, "When I am big I will go to school."

There are always points in every life when social forces reach out like strong hands to carry one into the main stream. The beginning of school is one of these high points.

So, if your child is saying "I won't!" when the time comes for the school bell to ring for him, something is wrong.

School itself, once he is enrolled, may change his feeling. But why wait until this happens? It may not happen.

How can we help our child to want to go to school?

From the time he is very young, look forward to the beginning of school for him with pleasant anticipation.

When you talk or read about school, remember that you want him to feel that it is a happy place. When you are out with him and walk past a school building, tell him a little of what is going on inside. If children's drawings or other schoolwork is visible at the windows, point them out to him as the children's achievements.

Interest and a good feeling about school should be planted in him by you long before he is of school age.

Your own feeling and attitude are important to him. Have you ever asked yourself how *you* feel about school?

Do you think of it as a place where children must do exactly as they are told, sit rigidly, work silently, and never question?

Do you think that teachers are different from other people?

Do you think of school as just something everyone has to go through?

Do you think of learning as something apart from living?

You yourself may have had a bad time at school— that is, you may have had a number of painful experiences there which somehow came to overshadow the greater number of pleasant experiences and the countless thrills of achievement and fulfillment.

If this is so, it may help you to remember that schools have changed a great deal and have become more humanized; that even though your own experiences left a bad feeling, many of the children who went to school with you enjoyed it. Some of them loved it so much that, when they grew up, they chose to become teachers.

Although your own child will have some bumpy times at school, as elsewhere, you want him to be able to cope with them, and to get over them quickly.

You want him to be stimulated and enriched by school, for that is its purpose.

If you have a negative, scornful, or hostile attitude toward schools, teachers, or learning, you are bound to convey the feeling to your child and influence him by it.

Our school system has no kindergarten, but begins with the first grade. Our daughter is now of school age, but my wife feels she is too young to attend. I disagree. Can you advise us?

Whether your community's educational system begins with the kindergarten or with first grade, your child should be entered at the stipulated age. Trust your daughter and do not hold her back. When others of her age are going to school, she wants and needs to go too. If you hold her back, she will feel left out of things. She will begin to feel that she is different from others and inferior to them. In such situations personality difficulties are frequently born.

When I was teaching first grade, I noticed a fine boy named Jimmy who seemed to enjoy school but was absent two, and sometimes even three, days a week. After each absence he returned with a note from his mother which said he had been ill. So far as I could see, he was a healthy and happy youngster. I observed him closely and could see no sign of ill health.

One day I telephoned Jimmy's mother to ask if I might visit her and her husband. She was hesitant but finally agreed. The date was set for an hour late in the evening when Jimmy would be in bed and asleep.

When I asked the boy's parents about his frequent absence from school, the father was surprised. He had known nothing about it. I sat quietly while he questioned his wife. Bit by bit the mystery was unveiled.

Jimmy was an only child, and his mother was having great emotional difficulty in accepting the fact that he was no longer a baby. She could not bear to have him away from her. While trying to keep him a baby, she was also giving him, because of her own dependence and love, responsibilities graver than she had any idea of. She had persuaded him to keep from his father any mention of the fact that she was making him stay home instead of attending school.

The wonderful boy responded to her request. He loved school, but cheerfully accepted the burden his mother laid upon him. He was helping her without, of course, realizing the sacrifice he was making.

Jimmy's mother had to have help in getting over her problem. She had taken a big step when she had consented to my visit. Then and there, talking with me on the phone, she had looked squarely at her problem.

She admitted on this evening that she had not had the courage to tell her husband about it, but the presence of Jimmy's teacher made it easier for her. I admired her, and still do. Not many people can face their own emotional problems as she did, with the determination to conquer them.

Jimmy attended school regularly after that. His mother became an active and valuable member of the parent-teacher association.

When your child is of school age, he is just as ready for school as all the other children. If you have doubts about this, do not worry your child but have a talk with the teacher or the principal. At home your own attitude should be one of confidence in your child and happy pride in the fact that he is going to school.

My first day at school was dreadful. How can I spare my child a similar experience?

Let me confess, first of all, that I had a very bad experience too. For months I had been looking forward to being big enough to go to school with my brothers and sisters. But as the time neared, I began to get a sinking feeling in my stomach. I was afraid to say anything about it. I thought that my brothers and sisters would call me a baby, and my parents would decide that I couldn't go because I wasn't big enough after all.

The night before the great day my mother was concerned about my lack of appetite and my silence. I wanted to go to bed early, and I am quite sure now that my mother didn't know whether to be pleased or worried because it was so unusual.

I was taken to school next morning by an older sister. As we walked the five blocks, she cautioned me about the things I must do to please my teacher. She took me to the classroom, where the teacher greeted me at the door. I walked bravely into the room, which seemed to me enormous. Within seconds I was feeling ill, and then, in front of the whole wide world, I brought up my breakfast! My sister was called to take me home.

Could any beginning be much worse? I remember vividly that little girl who was myself—her fright, her embarrassment, her misery. She suffered acutely.

Before I attempt to answer this question, let me tell you about Jerry.

Jerry had his fifth birthday in July. During the next few days he became very distressed. He was five years old now, a big boy. Why couldn't he go to kindergarten? Mother and Daddy had promised him he would go when he was five. What was wrong?

His parents did their best to explain that school began in September. He couldn't really grasp this.

During August Jerry's interest in school showed signs of fading, and his mother and father worked hard at building it up again. By the first of September he was talking excitedly about school. Daddy took him to the barber shop for a haircut. Mother took him shopping for a new suit and pair of shoes.

Jerry was proud of his new things. But on the Saturday before the opening of school he became very quiet. His parents were now doing most of the talking.

On Sunday Jerry seemed to be himself again, but in the evening he only pecked at his supper. He dawdled in preparing for bed. When he was tucked in and his mother said good night, he asked, "Will this be a long night?"

His mother took this to mean that he wanted the night to pass quickly because he could hardly wait until he was on his way to school.

On Monday morning Jerry rose promptly when his mother called him, and put on his new clothes. He ate a small breakfast and his mother wisely did not try to make him eat more.

When Jerry and his mother went out the door, Jerry suddenly stopped. He seemed frozen to the entrance of their home. He could not make himself go forward, or even back into the house. And then he vomited all over his new suit and shoes!

His mother lovingly comforted and soothed him, and was soon able to take him into the house. Jerry whispered to her, "At home I know where the bathroom is—" His mother said, "Do you know, I never thought of that! Of course you'd be worried! Never mind, we'll find out where it is just as soon as we get there."

His mother helped him to wash and change his

clothes. When he was all dressed, Jerry looked up at her with his bright smile and said, "Let's go!"

In Jerry's experience, and my own, lie answers to the question. It was an attack of "stage fright" that we suffered. Tension mounted to a spasm of fear so great that the body could not endure it, and revolted with nausea, a cold sweat, and vomiting. Some children, in this situation, burst into terrified panic-sobbing. Some wet themselves.

You can help your child get off to a good start.

Several months before school opens, begin to talk about it, casually. Drop or change the subject when your child's attention wanders. Do not insist that he listen because he is going to have to listen to teacher in school, or because you are telling him something for his own good, or anything like that.

Relax. Show no anxiety or tension. When you talk about school do not lecture about what he will have to do or how he should behave. Let there be no must's, do's or don't's. They are not in the least necessary, and will only frighten him.

Take walks with him to the school building, and answer his questions simply. You want the building to be familiar to him. Try to time some of these walks to arrive about five or ten minutes after school is out. You may then take him into the building for a minute or two, show him where the lavatory is, and let him know that he can always leave the room when he has to go.

Let him understand also that the teacher is there

to help him, and that he will like her and she will like him.

Do not buy him new clothes for the first day. There is so much "newness" for him in going off to school, why add to it? Let him wear clothes he likes, that he feels comfortable in, and that are already a part of him.

If he wants to take a favorite toy to kindergarten, by all means let him. He may forget to bring it home. If he does, do not scold, but just remind him of it. If he keeps on forgetting, forget about it yourself. He may have lost it or it may have become a part of his school equipment.

If tension is building up in your child before he begins school, or in fact at any other time of approaching climax, you will detect it by small signs such as loss of appetite, dawdling, unusual silence. The last often alternates with seemingly senseless bursts of temper.

You know by such signs that you yourself must relax first of all. Only then can you talk casually and pleasantly about what is to come. Your reassuring attitude will help your child bring out the questions he has. It is when tension and fear make him keep them to himself that molehills become mountains.

How can we help our child do well in school?

First, by having confidence in him.

Second, by being at home when he starts off to and

returns from school. He needs the assurance of your presence and your welcome each day.

Third, by admiring his new achievements and encouraging his new interests.

Fourth, by being actively interested in his school experiences. At first he probably won't talk much about them. Tell him what has been going on at home while he has been away at school, and how much you missed him. In return, he may think of things to tell you. Do not ask him, "What did you do in school today?" His answer would likely be, "Nothing." (The five-to-eight-year-old cannot report easily.) Ask him something specific, such as "Did you sing that new song today?" or "Did you play a new game?" Of course, the more you know about what is going on in kindergarten or whatever grade he is in, the more to the point your friendly questions will be. Try to get to know your child's school. Ask at the principal's office whether there is a written or printed curriculum you can see. Join the parent-teacher association, and try to attend any school affairs to which parents are invited.

Fifth, by encouraging your child to bring his school friends home, and to visit those of them you feel are good friends for him.

Here I must tell you of something I overheard one day. Two boys were standing on the front steps of the school building. John, a third-grader, was giving his younger friend the following advice:

"Bill, don't ever tell your mother about stuff like

reading and adding and spelling. If you do, she'll keep after you about them. Just tell her about things like drawing and singing, and the teacher, and games. Then she won't bother you, and she'll let you go out and play. You just listen to me and you'll be O. K."

Young children may receive many such tips from their older friends. They accept or reject them, usually without second thought. If your relationship with your child is warm, interested, and friendly, an "antiparent" tip will mean nothing to him. I am happy to say that this was the case with Bill. He admired John and was flattered by his attentions—but he did not take his advice because it made no sense to him. His mother was not an enemy; she was his friend.

Can we or should we rely entirely upon the teacher to help our child if he seems to be having difficulties?

Rely upon the teacher and your child until you are quite certain that there is some trouble that is not being cleared up. The teacher can be assumed to be doing her best, but there are many children in her class, and she may not know *your* child well enough to realize that he is not responding as he should.

Mrs. Stearns was very proud of her son George, a bright boy who seemed to have the qualities of a born leader. George had a wonderful time in kindergarten. Nothing was at all difficult for him, and he helped other children who were slow or awkward.

After he had entered the first grade, his mother observed that her son's interest in looking at books, listening to stories, and learning to read was diminishing. This seemed strange to her, because his interest had been high, and in the first grade children are taught to read. Shouldn't he now be excited and happy about learning to read?

At the end of the first month, Mrs. Stearns had a talk with George's teacher, who was surprised to learn that the boy's interest in books and reading had been high. She invited Mrs. Stearns to stay and visit the class.

In the reading lesson, the teacher held up words on cards. Mrs. Stearns saw that George could not recognize any of the words that he was called upon to read. She went home that day a very disheartened mother. She could not and would not believe that George had suddenly become stupid—and yet, why hadn't he recognized those simple words? He knew them, used them, and some of them he had once been able to recognize in his own books.

That evening when George was asleep, Mrs. Stearns discussed the matter with her husband. The problem seemed insoluble. They tried to figure out what errors they might have made in what they had taught George before he entered the first grade. But they could think of nothing that offered a clue. With her husband questioning her like a detective, Mrs. Stearns described several times in great detail her visit to the class that morning. All that emerged was the fact that George was surrounded by much bigger boys who also could not read the words on the cards. Mrs. Stearns then recalled that although George did not talk about school, he did talk with enthusiasm about the friends he played with— and from his talk it now seemed to her that they were all older boys.

Mr. and Mrs. Stearns could not make much of this but kept it in mind. Mrs. Stearns had more conferences with George's teacher, and also with the school principal. All three decided to observe the boy as best they could without disturbing him. In the evenings Mr. Stearns participated in his son's activities, and they would talk, the father following his son's lead and listening to him.

In a couple of weeks, they found the solution.

George had a nagging desire to be a great big boy. His heroes were baseball and football stars. From the age of six he had been trying to join in the games of older boys. In the first grade, he promptly made friends with the biggest boys there. Three of them, the largest and oldest in the class, were repeating first grade because they had not learned to read. Their feeling about reading was that it was "sissy stuff." It was a sour-grapes attitude, of course, probably rooted in embarrassment. But George could not know this. He was not even aware that he had adopted their attitude.

It was decided that George should be transferred to another first-grade class. His teacher announced the change to George in this way: "Miss Baird and the children in her first-grade room need you to help them because you are a big boy."

George was proud and happy to make the change. And luck was with him—and with his "team" of parents, teachers, and principal. For, as it turned out, he was the tallest boy in Miss Baird's class. Within a few days, he was working hard at learning to read, and from then on his progress was rapid.

Parents know their children in ways the school cannot know them. The teachers, on the other hand, know "their" children in ways the parents do not—by their revealed abilities, interests, and cooperation in work and play with many other children.

School and home were once separate worlds. Now they are working together more and more, helping and supplementing each other. There are, of course, still parents who make teachers bristle, and teachers who have much the same effect on parents when they come together over a problem concerning a child.

I take this opportunity to beg both sides to be tactful and to respect each other. You are working together for the child.

Nowadays there is happily less and less need for this reminder. When a child is going to school, a three-way friendship is established—based on integrity and respect—between parents, the child, and the teacher.

There will be few problems that such a team cannot solve.

How seriously should we take the report card?

The report card is a significant communication sent to the parents by the teacher. It cannot tell the whole story of what your child is doing in school. It is only indicative. Take it seriously, but—

Do not let that report card come between you and your child.

Do not make him afraid to bring it to you if its news is bad.

If it informs you that your child is failing or falling far behind in one subject or another, talk it over with him. Say something like this: "It seems that you're having some trouble with arithmetic (or whatever it is). Is it hard for you?" Let your child explain as well as he can, and listen sympathetically. He may then and there reveal where his difficulties lie, and you may be able to help him.

He may not be able to explain. He may not respond at all, because of embarrassment or fear. Do not press him. Praise him, instead, for his good work. This you should do anyway, of course. Well-earned praise is the best kind of encouragement.

Go to the school and discuss the low marks with

the teacher. Find out exactly how you can help your child in the areas where he is weak. The teacher, in turn, may learn something from you which will help her in working with him in the classroom.

No matter what the report says, always let your child feel you are with him. If he does fail in some subject, do not make him feel that he has failed *you*. He hasn't. His school work is your joint responsibility, and a most important one. Give him the feeling that you are there to help him.

Our child is a brilliant student, but it sometimes seems to us that he works too hard. Should we try to slow him down?

You cannot slow him down, just like that. His pace and his standards are set, and are acting upon him like a machine that drives him on and on. Give him every possible assurance, in every way you can, that you love him for himself. Try to be with him more, and ask for his company, but not as a demand or an order.

You may not get anywhere, because of the machine-like power of the forces within him. But if he is really working too hard, the strain is bound to tell. Be ready to help him when the opportunity offers.

Nora, a sweet and lovely girl, seemed suddenly a different child after her tenth birthday. She became aggressive toward her friends and her family. Her remarks took on a sharp tone and her whole manner became harsh. When she was even mildly corrected by her parents, she would burst into tears and run to her room. Her record in school had always been excellent. Now she seemed to have difficulty in getting her work done, for she was driving herself.

Nora's parents kept trying, unsuccessfully, to open the way for her to talk about her troubles.

At the end of the school year Nora did not come directly into the house with her report card. She stayed out in the yard until she had to come in to dinner. Nora's parents saw at once that their daughter had been having a hard time with herself.

About halfway through dinner, Nora said, "I certainly am glad vacation is here. I couldn't have taken another day of school!"

"I thought you liked school," her father said softly.

Nora began to cry helplessly, and this time she responded to her parents' gentleness and love. The floodgates burst open.

The child had set such high standards for herself that she could not possibly meet them. The goal she had set was to be best in everything, not only in studies but in all the activities. She just had to sing the solo in the school chorus, be president of the school council, win the spelling contest—the list went on and on.

When Nora showed her report card to her parents, they were justly proud of her record. But she herself was crushed because she had missed one big problem in her final arithmetic examination—through carelessness, she said. It had lowered her mark in this subject for the year from an *A* to an *A*-minus. She couldn't get over it. She felt disgraced.

It took a long time for Nora's parents to help her gain perspective. They kept pointing out that her record was most unusual, exceptionally high, and always had been. Little by little they helped her understand that she could not be the first and best in everything, and should not strive to be; and that because she was driving herself so hard in every direction, she had not been able to sit back and think of what she really liked and wished to master and excel in.

Now and then Nora rejected what they said and withdrew into herself. She had been working so hard and so blindly for so long that it was extremely difficult for her to change. But gradually she sifted and weighed her many activities and interests and found which ones meant more to her than others. By the time school opened again, Nora had set a new goal—to find herself, her real interests, through discovering and accepting her limitations.

The competitive drive is powerful, and those who succumb to it wholly can become its victims. It strikes some children harder than others, and at different ages. Competition is too often used to the point of abuse by both parents and teachers. Many children have gone down because they couldn't stand the pace. They have given up, not because they wanted to, but because it really was too much for them, and have resigned themselves with inner bitterness and anguish to being "fail-

ures." When you are a failure you don't have to compete any more—but you do not enjoy being a failure.

When Nora's parents told me of their daughter's
crisis, they said it was the most difficult, delicate, and
complicated situation that had ever confronted them.
They could not bear to see their daughter so unhappy.
They had concealed their own pain and foreboding from
her. With quiet sympathy they had helped her to see
that she had a problem, to feel their confidence that she
would solve it, and to know that they loved her first
and foremost for herself—entirely apart from her ac-
complishments, proud though they were of her triumphs.

I marvel that they could do this, and I respect
them. Understanding parents are truly sages and heroes.
They are great human beings—the Albert Schweitzers
and the Florence Nightingales of the home.

✳⤙✿⤚✳⤙✿⤙✳⤙✿⤙✳⤙✿⤙✳⤙✿⤚✳⤙✿⤚

TEN

Brothers and sisters

✳⤙✿⤚✳⤙✿⤙✳⤙✿⤙✳⤙✿⤙✳⤙✿⤚✳⤙✿⤚

A new baby is on the way. How should we tell our child?

Announce it as great good news for him personally and for all. Since it is family news, it should be announced when the members of the family are together.

I cannot tell you the words to say, because I am not you. And it would certainly not be helpful if I were to give you some sentences to memorize and to recite when the time comes. Such a recitation would be stilted, awkward, and unreal. I'm sure this is not what you want, even though you may think it is.

For your guidance, however, let me tell you about my friends Mr. and Mrs. Fuller, who carefully considered how to tell four-year-old Amy the big news. They

226

chose dinnertime to announce it—a good time. It was left to Mrs. Fuller, and it is a good idea for the mother to do the telling. She said, happily, "Amy, darling, you are going to have a new baby—a brother or sister. We don't know which yet."

They looked at her expectantly.

Amy stared at her mother and father. She seemed frightened. Then, in a scared little voice, she said, "Am *I* going to have a baby?"

They gasped. Children are sometimes utterly confounding! But they recovered almost immediately. They explained that Amy was not going to have a baby, that it was Mommy who was going to have it, but that it would belong to all of them. When she understood, the little girl was as happy and as excited as they had hoped. But they wonder to this day what Amy, at four, knew of babies—why she had been afraid.

The error these parents made was slight, but it does point up a rule that should be followed in such cases:

Be exact. Be accurate.

Sally and her mother were having malteds at the neighborhood drug store. Sally had been silent for a while. She was obviously thinking hard about something. At last she said, "Mommy, is the new baby inside getting a chocolate malted milk bath?"

Sally's mother almost choked over her drink. She could not help it, she had to laugh. But she finally managed to say, "I'm sorry, I didn't explain well. You see, the baby is in a kind of little nest or house inside, all cozy and separate from everything else."

Young children are visual-minded. They think in pictures. Sally's mother had told her that the baby was growing in Mother's stomach.

Children do not ask questions that cannot be answered simply, directly, and accurately. Nor is there any reason why they should not be answered in this way.

There are parents who tell the child nothing at all, who do not even announce that a new baby is coming. The child, of course, senses that something important is being withheld from him. He is quite likely to become a very different child during this period, developing strong anxieties or fears.

It is very wrong to exclude him from news and information to which he has a right as a member of the family. You will want his full cooperation when the new baby arrives. And you will certainly want him to love his new brother or sister, and not feel that he or she is a sudden intruder. How can he cooperate if he has been made to feel that the new baby has nothing to do with him? How can he love the newcomer if he has been made to feel that the baby is more important to Mommy and Daddy than he is?

Stevie, five years old, brought his mother a clean diaper for his baby sister. She thanked him, and as she attended to the baby, he said, "Mom, what would you do if I wasn't here? It's a good thing God gave me to you because I sure come in handy!"

His mother solemnly agreed.

When a child makes such a remark, he is confident

of his secure place in the family, and because of this confidence he is proud and happy to help in every way he can.

I plan to have my mother at home while I am at the hospital, but my little boy says that he won't have her. He is behaving badly. What can I do?

Sit down and think things over.

First: Did you let your child in on the big news? Does he know now why you are going away, and how long you expect to be gone?

Second: Have you been answering his questions with the attitude that he has a right to ask them and to be answered?

Third: If he knows that you are going away to bring back a new baby, does he feel that he is losing, or has lost, his place in your heart? Has he been given to understand that from now on he will have to be a big boy? Remember, he cannot grow up all at once to become Big Brother.

Fourth: Is he fond of his grandmother?

When a new baby is coming, do not delay in enlisting your child's cooperation. There will be days when you may be feeling ill; if he knows why, he will not be frightened and he will try as best he can to be quiet and helpful under your direction.

Keep him informed as to when, or about when, the baby is expected, and of any plans that are being changed because of it. In casual and pleasant talk, you can build up the understanding that the arrival date is not being deliberately set by Mother to interfere or compete with anyone. If a planned activity has to be postponed or given up entirely, let the family talk about it together so that all are joined in the spirit of working in a cause of happy mutual concern and responsibility.

When you make the arrangements for your child's care while you are away at the hospital, talk about them. If there are choices to be made, let your child have his say about them. He may, for example, prefer Aunt Mary to Grandmother.

When the arrangement is made, it should be talked about as something pleasant. You will be making remarks of this kind: "When Grandmother is here, you will have fun making cookies with her." You will not say: "If you aren't good when Grandmother is here, she won't let you watch TV."

Be considerate of Grandmother, or whoever it may be. Her services simply cannot be measured. If she makes mistakes, if she doesn't do things the way you do them, be understanding.

Your child is going to be troubled and upset while you are gone. Not all the time of course, but Daddy and whoever you put in charge must be prepared for this. A new book, a doll, a puzzle, a scrapbook, or a new record disk given the child about halfway through

Mother's absence, will help him. Daddy should try to telephone home each day; the days are going to be very long for his child.

There should be cooperative planning for the time when Mother comes home with the new baby. Everything should be carefully arranged in advance, to cover the first two weeks of her return. Check the following points:

1. Who will do the marketing?
2. Who will do the cooking?
3. Who will feed, bathe, and look after the child or the other children?
4. Who will do the cleaning?
5. Who will assume leadership until you can gradually take over yourself?

Grandparents can be helpful if they are willing, if they are not domineering, and if they are well enough to enjoy the lively company of a growing child.

A practical baby nurse is excellent for a new baby, but cannot be expected to take on all the household duties as well.

If you are not able to assume alone the complete care of the new baby, a good maid, under your direction, can do the rest.

On your return you will probably find yourself weak and tired. All the same, make every effort to let your child understand that you missed him while you were away, and that you love him just as much as ever. Introduce him to his new brother or sister so that he can see how tiny and helpless the new baby is, and he will begin to understand the cautions you are going to have to insist upon.

These cautions are, in fact, responsibilities which every member of the family shares with you. If you have done well, they accept the responsibilities whole-heartedly, with love and understanding. Your own cares are lightened when the new baby draws everyone closer together.

While I was busy with my new son this morning, Betty, our four-year-old, cut off all her curls. Now she won't be seen without her cap on. What should I do?

Betty is upset by what she did, and feels, moreover, that she looks awful. So don't scold her. I'm quite sure that Betty doesn't look awful, but the "awfulness" is within her. Take her to the beauty parlor to have her hair styled.

Betty has probably been feeling hurt because of the new baby. She may have cut her hair in order to get more attention from you and her father. Rather than dwell upon the incident, take it as notice that Betty needs more love and reassurance. Try to make more time for her, for playing and talking with her alone.

It is often very hard for the first child to accept the

new one. He once had first place; now he is second, or
at least has to share the affection on which he once had
the monopoly. He need not be marked as second. Do
everything that you can to make him feel that there is
no "first" or "second" but that there is plenty of love
to go around.

What is meant by "sibling rivalry"?

"Siblings" is just another way of saying brothers and/or
sisters. "Sibling rivalry" is the feeling of competition
that may exist between the children in the family. It is
a common problem. Even when the first child is fond
of the newcomer, he may feel a threat to his own security. He was once *the* child of the family. He now has
to adjust to the fact that he is no longer the one and
only. He may become competitive, fighting in many
ways for your love and attention.

Try to see the situation from his point of view.
For him, everything has changed with the arrival of the
new baby. The family schedule is different. He can no
longer have all the time he wants with Mother, or
clatter in and out freely. Even your attitude has changed.
In many ways, I am sure, he was your "baby." Now
there is a real baby, and you are expecting him to be
Big Brother, or her to be Big Sister.

If you find yourself doing a lot of scolding, nag-

ging, or shouting because he is misbehaving, sit down
and try to figure out why. Something is wrong. Your
child is probably misbehaving in order to get attention.
Even reproachful attention is better to him than none.

Help him in every way you can, so that he can
make his great adjustment with a minimum of pain and
trouble.

Here is a dramatic incident from the life of a six-year-
old which is still fresh in the mind of the same person,
now turned sixty.

At the end of his first semester in grade school, his
name was read out as one of those who had passed to
the upper half of the grade. When school was out, he
ran like a streak for home, pounded up three flights of
stairs, burst into the house and shouted, "Mama! Mama!
I—"

Mama, rising quickly from beside the cradle where
she was rocking the baby, shushed him.

The little boy was crushed. Evidently his excellent
achievement meant nothing to his mother. All she cared
about was the baby! If he had not happened to be a
gentle and responsible little boy, his mother might have
found him later hacking at a piece of furniture, or something like that. Instead, she found him sitting quietly—
too quietly—under the sink, of all places! She smiled at
him as if it were perfectly natural for him to be sitting
there, and said, "We didn't want to wake the baby, because if we did wake her, she'd cry and make such a
fuss that we wouldn't be able to hear ourselves think.

So now—tell me what wonderful thing happened to you. I can hardly wait to know."

She was skillful with that "we" touch—"*We* don't want the baby to wake and interrupt our talk with her crying." She thought that made the "shush" a partnership. Actually it had not, as far as he was concerned.

This adult, as I pointed out, remembers every detail of the incident. It seems a trivial thing in a lifetime, yet it undoubtedly caused more real suffering than the person it happened to can ever know. If the mother hadn't realized instantly how she had pulled the carpet from under those eager little feet, the result would have been more serious, of course. The boy might have turned his bitterness against his baby sister, and these two siblings would have grown up in destructive competition.

Some siblings are actually pitted against each other by their parents.

"Why can't you be as good as your sister is?" "Don't tell me you can't do this—your brother can, and he's younger than you are." Have you ever heard such words of "encouragement"? Parents who do this have the best intentions, but what they are really doing is encouraging disastrous competition and jealousy.

Among siblings, competition can become a state of warfare, hot or cold. Each tries to triumph over or score off the other in every way he can find. The parents become the "generals" in this state of war. Sometimes they compete too, taking the side of one child against the other, and against each other.

Competition in a family drives its members apart. Each becomes a separate unit, fighting for his place in the sun. No one is the better or the happier for this.

The happy family is a unit to which each member contributes his best because he can and because he wants to—because he does not feel threatened, afraid, bitter, or insecure.

When the new baby arrives, do not forget or neglect the important emotional needs of your growing child. Help him to feel happy that he now has a brother or sister. Let him feel that nothing has been taken from him, but that something has been added to enrich his life. He will respond.

My first child is very affectionate, but the younger one is cold and discourages any show of affection. Is something different about my second child?

No two children are alike. Even twins are not exactly alike.

When one child wants and enjoys a lot of petting and hugging, and the other doesn't, it is sometimes hard for the parents to keep from developing a coolness toward the youngster who is not openly demonstrative. Everyone loves to be loved, and feels hurt when someone turns away from a kiss or a hug, or merely tolerates it.

Each child has his distinctive personality, and it begins to be seen early. One baby is very "good"—he gives no trouble, and everything goes like clockwork. The second is entirely different, and may fuss and cry and get you up at all hours. Why? Because, among other reasons, each is himself and not anyone else.

The child who does not welcome demonstrative affection is not rejecting you. Nor is he queer or unusual. He has his own way of loving. Accept the fact, and do not withdraw or lessen your love because of it.

See to it that he is getting his full share of your interest in him as an individual, and respect his wishes.

Why is it so hard for children to take turns talking?

It is easier for many people to talk than to listen. This is particularly true of children, for they relate everything to themselves, and only gradually grow into broader interests. To listen is to give oneself over to another person, in the sense of being interested in him rather than in oneself.

When you think about it, listening does seem quite an attainment. Many times you listen to someone without really listening. You are not interested. You think about other things.

Mealtimes—dinner especially, when the family is together—are among the best times for training and guiding your child in both talking and listening.

At dinner, each member of the family has before him the whole family audience. The children are stimulated by this fact, and usually each of them has so much to tell and so much to ask about! The result is sometimes a kind of free-for-all with each child trying to say everything he can. There may be three, four, or five voices all talking or shouting eagerly at the same time, with nobody listening to anybody else.

Why not discuss this with your children and together lay down some rules?

1. Everyone must have his turn, but he must not abuse it by holding the floor too long.

2. No one can have a second turn until all the others have had their first turn.

3. A turn is entirely one's own. An exchange of opinions, or a comment, does not count as a turn.

4. No one should be deprived of a turn as a punishment because he has done something wrong that day. To sit through a happy family meal feeling oneself an outcast is a cruel experience.

5. If someone has something to say which he feels is of great importance or urgency, let him announce the fact. Give him precedence. If it turns out not to be so important as to deserve the first turn, he will know it by the way it is received. It will fall flat. In this way each child will begin to become aware of the difference between important and less important matters, and will begin to weigh and judge what is important.

If chaos still reigns? Then—

6. Make a schedule or plan of turns. To be fair, this plan should rotate daily. The eldest child should not always have first turn, nor the youngest always wait until everyone else has had his say. Mother and Daddy should of course be included in the plan.

If you try these suggestions, you are going to hatch your own ideas for the plan, and so will everyone in the family. Whatever they are, fair play should be the basic rule.

A plan can be great fun. It must be a workable compromise between the rigid and the fluid, between letter and spirit. The ideal is informality plus fair shares.

Training and guidance in talking and listening can and should be an everyday affair. At all times the older child should be discouraged from belittling or laughing at the ideas, opinions, or expressions of the younger. He should instead be encouraged to respect them as the same kind of growing that he himself did, and which, on his own level, he is still doing.

My friends the Lawtons have four children, and all the members of this family are lively, interesting, and talkative. Little Janet was rather a silent child, for a Lawton. One evening at dinner when talk had been in full swing for some time, her small voice rose above all the others, shrill and piping:

"Oh, for heaven's sake! Can't I ever say something?"

After a startled second there came a burst of delighted laughter from her family. It was followed by a quick apology from Daddy. "Janet, you're right. I guess we forgot, because you've got a soft voice. If we forget again, just remind us. Now it's your turn."

Janet had an interesting experience to tell about, and she told it well. The Lawtons could not possibly have made or adhered to any plan—but from then on, Janet always had her turn.

Our nine-year-old has become very bossy toward her sister. The younger one is beginning to resent it. How can we clear this up?

In casual talks with the older child, explain as simply and clearly as possible her young sister's feelings. Give her at the same time something to do with her sister by which she can guide or lead without bossing.

Explain that young children need advance notice, in a pleasant manner, of what they are to do next, because they cannot be pushed into doing things. Explain also your own techniques of guidance, which are based on respect for the individual and understanding of his limitations. Not always but frequently, a break-out of bossiness in the children is a reflection of bossy parental behavior.

Do not scold your older child or forbid her to play

with her sister. In being aggressive she is testing power
—but she is also trying to be grown-up, helpful, and
important. By taking her into your confidence, instead
of thwarting a natural desire you show her how to use
authority with consideration and responsibility. She can
be very helpful indeed! She is also going to begin to
understand the techniques that Mother and Daddy use
with her—the why and the how of them. This understanding can make her increasingly cooperative, and appreciative of all that you do for her.

Between the ages of nine and twelve, many children
try to boss younger brothers and sisters. The nine-year-
old is entering an in-between stage. He is no longer a
young child, yet he is far from grown. He is beginning
to question the parental authority—at the same time he
wants to use authority himself.

Let him have some authority, but help him to use
it well. Teach him that authority is not power but
responsibility. Authority must not be abused.

*Why does our nine-year-old son object to
being the oldest child? Shouldn't he be happy
about his place in the family?*

Some children, after the age of eight, grow so fast and
become so assured (seemingly) and generally useful that
the parents tend to forget they are still children. The

younger children in the family *look* like children, and because of this the older child does not. The parents, without realizing it, often demand too much of the eldest in the way of mature behavior.

Ten-year-old Donald was the first of the three West children. The two younger boys, aged five and three, looked up to their big brother. They adored him, and his parents had long known they could rely upon him to take care of them. Donald's mother led a busy and useful social life. She was active in many important community organizations.

One evening, when he was at home alone with his father, Donald remarked, "I don't think it's so good to be born too soon."

Mr. West was startled and puzzled by this remark, but felt there was something important behind it. "Maybe you're right," he said casually. "Sometimes it seems better to be younger rather than older. What do you think?"

As they talked, Mr. West gently probed and explored his son's feelings. He detected no note of complaint as such, but it was evident that Donald had a grievance and that it was valid.

Later that night, he and his wife took inventory of all that they had been asking of Donald. They had frequently called upon him to take care of his younger brothers. Sometimes the little ones were in his charge not only in the afternoon, when he came home from school, but in the evening as well, when the father and mother went out together. He had never objected.

Friends of his own age used to phone him, or to call him to come out and play. "I'm taking care of my little brothers," he would reply. Such calls were becoming rare. That afternoon, Donald had received and again turned down one of them. His mother had heard him and had thought nothing of it. But she realized now that Donald showed a lot of courage to speak up, to say something to his father.

The Wests faced this situation squarely, and themselves as well. They thought about all three of their children. The two small boys were as bright and lively as could be—the Wests found it hard to recall whether Donald, at their age, had been as lively. Had he always been so quiet and calm?

They then thought of all the other ten-year-olds they could. This too was hard, for they did not know any very well, except through other parents' talk. Donald had only a few friends who came to the house. They did remember, however, their pride in their fine, dependable son when other parents talked of difficulties with their nine- or ten-year-olds.

It occurred now to these self-searching, honest parents that Donald was too quiet, too calm, too dependable —that he was, in fact, subdued!

They became aware that they had been dominating him, to the extent of making use of him, and suspected that they had been doing this unconsciously for several years. He was such a cooperative and responsible boy that they could not now remember the last time he had ever said "No!" or "I won't!" or "I can't!"

They knew, of course, that they couldn't very well say to their son the very next morning at breakfast: "Donald, we have been asking too much of you. Beginning right now, you are free to do as you wish." That would disturb him, deeply. He would feel lost.

Both parents gave up some of their activities. When Donald came back from school day after day, expecting to be given charge of his brothers, he found his mother there, making no preparations to go out. And at night, after his father came home, they all stayed home. The parents explained that they were giving up this and that because they had taken on too much outside the house and had been tiring themselves out. They told the children that they wanted one going-out night in the week, and asked Donald if he would mind helping with the younger boys that night.

They watched to see what Donald would do with his free time. They had resolved to help him if he seemed to need help.

Within a month Donald was a much more outgoing child. His relationship with his younger brothers became more interesting—he had new ideas of things for them to do, and some of them were very good activities.

In good time—in just the nick of time, for him—Donald became a real ten-year-old. He was more mature than most, but he developed a sense of humor and of fun. He had looked sober, almost dull. Now he looked happy.

I have spent a long time on Donald's story not only because it may help you if you yourself have a Donald, but also because I wish to pay homage to all the wonderful parents who know, become aware of, and use the magic of love, respect, and consideration in bringing up their children.

elevenELEVEN

✽↝✿↝✽↝✿↝✽↝✿↝✽↝✿↝✽↝✿

"My children"

✽↝✿↝✽↝✿↝✽↝✿↝✽↝✿↝✽↝✿

In the same way that many parents have asked me to
answer questions about their children's problems, children have shared with me many of their wishes,
thoughts, and experiences.

From observing children and talking with them I
have learned a great deal about what they think and
believe. I have learned too that parents and teachers
make a big mistake when they underestimate the young
child's ability to think and to express his thoughts.

One morning when the children were in the nursery
school playground, Eddie came from the sandbox to sit
on the bench beside me.

"Some day," he confided, "I will be a big man. I
will be a daddy to a little boy and a little girl. I won't

live at home with a mommy, though. I won't get mad like some daddies do. We will play together, and on Sunday we will have breakfast together. This is what will happen when I am a big man. We won't need a mommy around."

I assured him that he would grow up to be a fine big man and a wonderful daddy. He climbed into my lap and gave me a hug and a kiss. Then he jumped down, ran over to his tricycle, and was off to a happy morning.

Eddie, of course, was having trouble at home, and I learned later that his mother and father were quarreling. Right now, all he needed—and all he was asking for from me—was reassurance.

I would have done wrong if I had tried to probe, asking him what was really bothering him—or if I had said that he must always love his mother and his father —or if I had insisted that when he grew up to be a daddy he was going to have to share his little boy and his little girl with a mommy. A lecture, an argument, or a cross-examination would only have disturbed him more.

When a child is troubled or fearful, he wants to be physically close, if only for a minute, to one he can trust, and to confide in this person, feeling that he will be understood. He needs this kind of reassurance in order to maintain his balance and self-confidence.

A good teacher does not interfere or come in any way between children and parents.

Some trees grow very straight and tall.
Other trees prefer to stay low and small.

There are trees that are big and round,
And there are others that are thin and flat.

Cindy made this observation and dictated it to me
—developing it as she went along—when she was six
years old and in the first grade. I did not try to discuss
it with her, but praised her for it, saying it was a big
thought with a lot of things in it.

Several weeks later she came to me to talk about it
some more. She had concluded that "trees grow like
people grow." "Each tree is different," she explained.
"Each person is not like anybody else." She finished by
wondering why God did not make all people alike, and
all trees the same.

She did not ask me for the answer, and I was pleased
about that. Cindy was thinking very hard, and would
go on thinking. I hoped that one day she would bring
me the answer she had figured out all by herself.

She did, and it did not take her very long. She decided that it would not be very interesting, or quite
right, if everything and everyone were the same size,
shape, and color.

When she explained she said, "I wouldn't like it
that way at all. Would you?"

I said that I wouldn't like it either.

"So now, you see," Cindy reassured me, "God
knows what he is doing."

It was Sunday morning and breakfast time at the
Bradfords'. Mrs. Bradford served five-year-old Eleanor

Jane's favorite cereal, and as a surprise she had sliced peaches over it—the first peaches of the season. Eleanor Jane loved peaches, but she did not plunge right in. She jumped down from her chair and went searching for a magazine she had been looking at a few days before. She couldn't find it, and everyone had to help; she was too intent and excited to be able to explain why she must have this magazine at this time. What had been meant to be a relaxed and leisurely Sunday breakfast took on something of a frantic air.

But at last the magazine was found. Eleanor Jane turned the pages, and there it was—a full-page advertisement in color of the same cereal in a bowl with fresh sliced peaches arranged on it in a pinwheel effect.

Eleanor Jane returned to the table, and she and her mother rearranged the peach slices in all the bowls of cereal, and then they all began their breakfast. When Eleanor Jane had finished the last spoonful, she looked up at her quietly amused parents and said, with a sign of satisfaction, "My! That was the best breakfast I ever had!"

Which reminds me of six-year-old Carl. We were having lunch, and I had asked Carl to dish out the peas on each plate while I served the rest of the food. With the serving spoon Carl formed on each of the three plates a letter with the peas. He made an *F* for Frances on mine, an *M* for Mary on Mary's plate, and a *C* for himself. By the time we sat down to eat, the lunch was not as hot as it should have been, but Mary and I were proud of

Carl and his artistic achievement—and certainly Carl was proud and happy. We all felt, like Eleanor Jane, that this was the best meal we had ever had!

Linda, who is five, came to my home to visit with us one Saturday morning. I was busy in the kitchen whipping up an angel-food cake. She perched on the high kitchen stool and supervised. When the cake went into the oven she climbed down, and she suddenly turned wistful. "I wish it was like this at our house," she said. But then she stood up very straight and said, "But it is an awful lot of work, so Mother can't do it any more."

In the first remark she had expressed a deep-felt wish. In the second, she came to the defense of her mother, somehow realizing that there had been an accusation in her wish. She corrected herself, and put the world (me) right about it.

One day while at my window in the schoolroom, I heard a child's voice singing on and on, as merrily as a cricket. I looked out. A boy and a girl were playing in a large sandbox near my window. The little girl, who was singing, was very busy making sand cookies. The boy also was busy, working very hard at making a huge sand hill. He was silent at his work.

Suddenly he looked up at the little girl and asked, "Why do you sing so much?"

The girl looked at him for a second. Then she explained seriously, "I've got to sing when I'm happy, and you can't make anything come out right unless you're happy."

When I was coming home one day in the late afternoon, I saw Evelyn, the seven-year-old who lives next door, sitting on the steps of her house. She looked up at me and nodded, but there was such beauty in her face that I just could not go on. I stood beside her for a few minutes. She was watching the sunset, and that alone was worth stopping for, although in my grown-up absorption in other things I had not noticed how really beautiful it was.

It began to fade. Evelyn, still in her private world, looked up at me with eyes that seemed to reflect the glory of the sunset. "There must be a God," she said. "No one else could make the sky so pretty."

These children, and the many others you have met in this book, are not mine, of course. What they have given me, in pleasure and joy, in sharing and understanding, is mine. I see thousands of faces. Some are briefly troubled or angry, some are tightened or strained by fears to which they cannot give a name, some are a little too old for their years and some a little too young.

But all are beautiful.

These children give so much to the adults who are privileged to be with them! I know of no better way of growing than to grow with children. For the truth is, as I believe, that most of us grownups are not really grown up. There is no end to growing.

I offer this book to parents in deepest appreciation of their great work. If it has in it, and explains well, some of the magic that children have taught me, it may, here and there, help a growing grownup and a growing child.

INDEX

※↩✿↝※↩✿↝※↩✿↝※↩✿↝※↩✿

253

ABOUT THE AUTHOR

DR. FRANCES R. HORWICH, popularly known as Miss Frances of Ding Dong School, has received more than 60 awards and citations, including three Emmy Award nominations, television's top award for the best children's educational program; the *Look* Magazine Award two years in a row for the best children's program; the Associated Press Award as the Woman of the Year in Education; the George Foster Peabody Award; the *Parents' Magazine* Award; the Sylvania TV Award for the outstanding juvenile program; the Christopher Award; and the Book of Knowledge Award as the Woman of the Year in Education. She has taught and lectured at the University of California, Northwestern University, the University of North Carolina, and many others. Northwestern University has established the Frances R. Horwich Scholarships.